Equality and Diversity
in the
Lifelong Learning Sector

Equality and Diversity
in the
Lifelong Learning Sector

Second edition

Ann Gravells and Susan Simpson

Los Angeles | London | New Delhi
Singapore | Washington DC

Learning Matters
An imprint of SAGE Publications Ltd
1 Oliver's Yard
55 City Road
London EC1Y 1SP

SAGE Publications Inc
2455 Teller Road
Thousand Oaks, California 91320

SAGE Publications India PVT LTD
B1/I 1 Mohan Cooperative Industrial Area
Malthura Road
New Dehli 110 044

SAGE Publications Asia-Pacific Pte Ltd
3 Church Street
#10–04 Samsung Hub
Singapore 049483

© 2012 Ann Gravells and Susan Simpson

First published in 2009
Reprinted in 2009, 2010 and 2011
Second edition published in 2012

Library of Congress Control Number: 2012931687

British Library Cataloguing in Publication Data

A catalogue record for this book is available from the British Library

Editor: Amy Thornton
Development Editor: Jennifer Clark
Production Controller: Chris Marke
Project Management: Deer Park Productions
Marketing Manager: Catherine Slinn
Cover Design: Topics
Typeset by: Pantek Media
Printed by: MPG Books, Bodmin, Cornwall

ISBN: 978 0 85725 849 6
ISBN: 978 0 85725 697 3 (pbk)

CONTENTS

ACKNOWLEDGEMENTS

Ann and Susan would like to thank Billy Harrison and Caroline Beeson Spence for their support and contributions while working on the second edition of this book. Feedback from readers of the previous edition of this book has also been extremely valuable.

A special thank you goes to both our families for their never-ending support and patience as well as their excellent proofreading skills.

Thanks also go to the staff and students of the teacher training departments at Bishop Burton College and North East Lincolnshire Council Community Learning Services.

Every effort has been made to trace the copyright holders and to obtain their permission for the use of copyright material. We will gladly receive any information enabling us to rectify any error or omission in subsequent editions.

The authors welcome any comments; please contact them via Ann Gravells' website: www.anngravells.co.uk.

 **Ann Gravells** is a lecturer in teacher training at Bishop Burton College in East Yorkshire and a consultant to The University of Cambridge Institute of Continuing Education's Assessment Network. She has been teaching since 1983.

She is an external quality consultant for the City & Guilds teacher training qualifications, a presenter of events and a consultant for various other projects.

Ann is a director of her own company Ann Gravells Ltd, an educational consultancy which specialises in teaching, training and quality assurance. She delivers events and courses nationwide.

Ann holds a Masters in Educational Management, a PGCE, a Degree in Education, and a City & Guilds Medal of Excellence for teaching. Ann is a Fellow of the Institute for Learning and holds QTLS status.

She is often asked how her surname should be pronounced. The 'vells' part of Gravells is pronounced like 'bells'.

She is the author of:

- *Achieving your TAQA Assessor and Internal Quality Assurer Award*
- *Delivering Employability Skills in the Lifelong Learning Sector*
- *Passing PTLLS Assessments*
- *Preparing to Teach in the Lifelong Learning Sector*
- *Principles and Practice of Assessment in the Lifelong Learning Sector*
- *What is Teaching in the Lifelong Learning Sector*

She is the editor of:

- *Study Skills for PTLLS*

 **Susan Simpson** is a teacher in teacher training at the North East Lincolnshire Council's Community Learning Services in Grimsby. She has been teaching since 1980.

Susan is Head of Community Learning Services and has been a curriculum manager for Education and Training, ICT and Business Administration and Law for five years. She developed, managed and taught adult education programmes in Botswana for ten years. Susan has also presented at regional level for teacher training and nationally for ICT Skills for Life.

Susan holds a Post Graduate Diploma in Management Studies, BA (Hons) in Further Education and Training, and a Certificate in Education (Hons) in Business Studies and Economics.

Ann and Susan have co-authored:

- *Equality and Diversity in the Lifelong Learning Sector*
- *Passing CTLLS Assessments*
- *Planning and Enabling Learning in the Lifelong Learning Sector*

Ann and Susan welcome any comments from readers; please contact them via Ann's website. www.anngravells.co.uk.

In this chapter you will learn about the:

- structure of the book and how to use it

- Qualifications and Credit Framework (QCF)

- professional teaching standards

The structure of the book and how to use it

This book has been specifically written for anyone working towards the Certificate in Teaching in the Lifelong Learning Sector (CTLLS) or the Diploma in Teaching in the Lifelong Learning Sector (DTLLS). DTLLS is also known as The Certificate in Education (Cert Ed) or the Post Graduate Certificate in Education (PGCE).

Equality and Diversity is an optional unit of the qualifications; however, the content is applicable to anyone requiring further information to assist their teaching in an educational context, or for continuing professional development (CPD). It will support all teachers, tutors and trainers at any point in their own learning journey to embed equality and diversity within their practice.

Throughout the book the general term *student* is used to denote a learner or trainee etc. However, the term *learner* is used in direct quotations.

The book is structured in chapters which relate to the content of the *Equality and Diversity* unit. You can work logically through the book or just look up relevant aspects within the chapters which relate to areas of your teaching.

There is some repetition of content between the chapters due to its relevance to the particular chapter topic, for example the Equality Act 2010, inclusivity and discrimination. For the purpose of this book, the generic terms *teacher* and *student* are used. However, there are times when the word *learner* is used, for example in quotations used in chapters and the standards in the appendices.

There are activities to enable you to think about how you can embed and advance equality and diversity within your teaching, and examples to help you understand the subject. At the end of each section in Chapters 1–5 is an extension activity to stretch and challenge your learning further. Chapter 6 addresses most of the legislation, employment regulations, policies and codes of practice relevant to the promotion and advancement of equality and the valuing of diversity. All legislation is subject to change; therefore you are advised to check for any relevant updates or amendments. The content of the book does not constitute legal advice or guidance.

There is a cross-referencing grid towards the end of each chapter showing which areas of the Professional Teaching Standards and the Equality and Diversity assessment criteria have been covered.

The theory focus at the end of each chapter includes references and further information to enable you to research relevant topics by using text books, publications and the internet.

The appendices contain the Equality and Diversity unit criteria at levels 3 and 4, a list of relevant abbreviations and acronyms, a glossary of terms, and a checklist for promoting and advancing equality and diversity. The index at the back of the book will help you locate useful topics quickly and easily.

The content of the learning outcomes is the same at both level 3 and level 4; the difference in level is expressed in the amount of work you will be required to submit. For example, if you are taking level 3 you will *explain* how or why you do something, at level 4 you will *analyse* how or why you do it. If you are working towards level 4 you will need to carry out relevant research, reference your work to theorists, use other texts besides this one and use an academic style of writing.

If you are teaching nationally or internationally, some of the regulations and organisations referred to in the book may only be relevant in England. You are therefore advised to check what is current and applicable to the nation or country in which you work. The most recent legislation uses the term *advancing equality and diversity* instead of *promoting equality and diversity*. The intention is that actions you take will have an impact on your students and will help them progress and, as a result, achieve improved outcomes. This will be explained further throughout the book.

Qualifications and Credit Framework (QCF)

The QCF is a system for recognising skills and qualifications by awarding credit values to the units within the qualifications. A credit value of one equates to 10 learning hours. These values enable you to see how long it would take an average student to achieve a unit. For example, the *Equality and Diversity in the Lifelong Learning Sector* unit is 6 credits which equates to

60 hours. The total hours include *contact time* with a teacher and assessor, and *non-contact time* for individual study, assignment work and the production of a portfolio of evidence.

There are three sizes of qualifications with the titles:

- award (1 to 12 credits)

- certificate (13 to 36 credits)

- diploma (37 credits or more)

The terms award, certificate and diploma do not relate to progression, i.e. you don't start with an award, progress to a certificate and then a diploma. The terms relate to how big the qualification is (i.e. its size) which is based on the total number of credits. By looking at the title and credit value, you will be able to see how difficult it is and how long it will take to complete.

The difficulty of the qualification is defined by its level. The QCF has 9 levels: entry level plus 1 to 8 (there are 12 levels in Scotland).

A rough comparison of the levels to existing qualifications is:

- Level 1 – GCSEs (grades D–G)

- Level 2 – GCSEs (grade A*–C)

- Level 3 – A levels

- Level 4 – Vocational Qualification (VQ) level 4, Higher National Certificate (HNC)

- Level 5 – VQ level 5, Degree, Higher National Diploma (HND)

- Level 6 – Honours degree

- Level 7 – Masters degree

- Level 8 – Doctor of Philosophy (PhD)

All qualifications on the QCF use the terms *learning outcomes* and *assessment criteria*. The learning outcomes state what the *learner will do*, and the assessment criteria what the *learner can do*. Units can be *knowledge based* (to assess understanding), *performance based* (to assess competence) or a mixture of the two. Please see Appendices 1 and 2 for the Equality and Diversity learning outcomes and assessment criteria.

Ofqual together with its partner regulators in Wales – Department for Children, Education, Lifelong Learning and Skills (DCELLS) – and Northern

Ireland – Council for the Curriculum, Examinations and Assessment (CCEA) – is responsible for the regulation of the Qualifications and Credit Framework (QCF). There is a separate framework for Scotland. The frameworks will eventually contain all available qualifications in the country.

Lifelong Learning Professional Teaching Standards

In September 2007, standards came into effect for all new teachers in the Lifelong Learning Sector who teach or assess on government-funded programmes in England. This includes all post-16 education, including further education, adult and community learning, work-based learning and offender education. Please see the web links at the end of the chapter for Northern Ireland, Scotland and Wales.

Teachers in the Lifelong Learning Sector should value all students individually and equally. As a teacher you should be committed to lifelong learning and professional development, and strive for continuous improvement through reflective practice. The key purpose of being a teacher is to create effective and stimulating opportunities for learning, through high quality teaching that enables the development and progression of all students.

The standards encompass six domains:

A   Professional Values and Practice

B   Learning and Teaching

C   Specialist Learning and Teaching

D   Planning for Learning

E   Assessment for Learning

F   Access and Progression

If you are taking one of the teaching qualifications, you will need to meet all the relevant criteria relating to the *scope, knowledge* and *practice* required in your job role (referenced by: S for *scope*, K for *knowledge* or P for *practice* within the chapters of this book).

If the standards are applicable to your job role you may need to achieve a relevant teaching qualification such as the award in Preparing to Teach in the Lifelong Learning Sector (PTLLS) followed by either the CTLLS if you are an associate teacher or the DTLLS if you are a full teacher.

The Cert Ed and the PGCE have the same content as DTLLS. They are usually achieved via a university whereas DTLLS is achieved at a college or training organisation.

The associate teaching role carries significantly less than the full range of teaching responsibilities and does not require the teacher to demonstrate an extensive range of knowledge, understanding and application of curriculum innovation or curriculum delivery strategies. Think of this as teaching using materials that have been created by someone else.

The full teaching role carries the full range of teaching responsibilities and requires the teacher to demonstrate an extensive range of knowledge, understanding and application of curriculum innovation or curriculum delivery strategies. Think of this as teaching with materials you have created, such as a scheme of work, session plans, resources and presentations, etc.

The IfL is the professional body for teachers, trainers, tutors and trainee teachers in the Learning and Skills Sector in England. If you haven't already done so, you could register with the IfL via their website, www.ifl.ac.uk, to gain all the benefits of belonging to a professional body. The IfL has a *Code of Professional Practice* (2008) for all members to follow and you will need to keep up to date with developments in your subject area by partaking in CPD.

For the purpose of the teaching regulations in England, the Institute for Learning (IfL) definitions of associate and full teacher apply whether you are working on a full-time, part-time, fractional, fixed-term, temporary or agency basis.

Registering with the IfL, gaining the relevant qualification and maintaining your CPD will enable you to apply for your teaching *status*. This will be either: Associate Teacher Learning and Skills (ATLS) for *associate* teachers, or Qualified Teacher Learning and Skills (QTLS) for *full* teachers. This is a requirement under the Further Education Teachers' Qualifications (England) Regulations (2007). Further details regarding the associate and full teaching roles, together with how to apply for ATLS/QTLS can be found on the IfL website.

Summary

In this chapter you have learnt about the:

- structure of the book and how to use it
- Qualifications and Credit Framework (QCF)
- professional teaching standards

Theory focus

References and further information

Gravells, A and Simpson, S (2010) *Planning and Enabling Learning in the Lifelong Learning Sector* (2nd edn). Exeter: Learning Matters

Gravells, A (2012) *Preparing to Teach in the Lifelong Learning Sector* (5th edn). London: Learning Matters

IfL (2008) *Code of Professional Practice: Raising concerns about IfL members* (V2). London: Institute for Learning

LLUK (2006) *New Overarching Professional Standards for Teachers, Tutors and Trainers in the Lifelong Learning Sector*. London: Skills for Business

Websites

CCEA Northern Ireland – www.rewardinglearning.org.uk

DCELLS Wales – www.awarding.org.uk/public/stakeholders/dcells

Institute for Learning – www.ifl.ac.uk

National Institute for Adult Continuing Education – www.niace.org.uk

Professional Standards for Lecturers in Scotland's Colleges – http://tiny.cc/3w9jg

Professional Standards for Teachers, Tutors and Trainers in the Lifelong Learning Sector – http://tinyurl.com/4xkcz5z

Qualifications and Credit Framework – http://tinyurl.com/447bgy2

Scottish Credit and Qualifications Framework – www.scqf.org.uk

Teaching Qualifications for Northern Ireland – http://tiny.cc/2bexb

Introduction

In this chapter you will learn about:

- meanings and benefits of equality and diversity
- the Equality Act 2010
- promoting a positive culture

There are activities and examples which will help you reflect on the above and assist your understanding of the key features of a culture which promotes and advances equality and diversity. At the end of each section is an extension activity to stretch and challenge your learning further.

At the end of the chapter, there is a cross-referencing grid showing how the content of this chapter contributes towards the Professional Teaching Standards and the Equality and Diversity assessment criteria at levels 3 and 4. There is also a theory focus with relevant references, further information and websites you might like to refer to.

Meanings and benefits of equality and diversity

When teaching, you will have a group of students from different backgrounds and cultures and/or with different needs and abilities. You will therefore experience diversity as no two people will be the same. You can add value to your teaching by recognising the many differences your students have and incorporating their diverse experiences within your sessions. By combating discrimination, valuing diversity and advancing equality your students' outcomes should improve (i.e. what they will achieve). It should help to create a positive and equal learning environment.

You can help ensure your students are motivated and comfortable in their environment by being positive towards their needs, considerate and respectful. In doing so, you will encourage these qualities in your students and colleagues. If you have a student with a disability, don't label them as *disabled* but consider them as an individual with a variation in *ability*. Not all differences are visible and disability is an example of a difference which cannot always be seen. It is important not to make assumptions or stereotype your students. Conversations with students concerning their needs are essential to assess how best you can address those needs. Equal opportunities for all is only achievable when conversations with individuals take place to ascertain their needs which are then acted upon.

These variations are what make your students unique, and they shouldn't be excluded from the learning process as a result. Everyone is different in some way from others, and these differences should be celebrated and acknowledged to give equal opportunity to all.

Equality

Equality is about the rights of students to have access to, attend, and participate in their chosen learning experience. This should be regardless of ability and/or circumstances. Inequality and discrimination should be tackled to ensure fairness, decency and respect among students. Equality of opportunity is a concept underpinned by legislation to provide relevant and appropriate access for the participation, development and advancement of all individuals and groups.

In the past, equality has often been described as *everyone being the same* or *having the same opportunities*. Nowadays, it can be described as *everyone being different, but having equal rights*.

Diversity

Diversity is about valuing and respecting the differences in students, regardless of ability and/or circumstances, or any other individual characteristics they may have. If you have two or more students, you will experience diversity. You are also different from your students in many ways, and they are different from each other; therefore they are entitled to be treated with respect, with their differences acknowledged and needs taken into consideration.

Activity

Find out who is responsible for equality and diversity within your organisation, and whether any training is available which you could attend. Is there a positive culture towards equality and diversity within your organisation or do you feel some things could be changed? If so, why?

The Government's *Equality Strategy – Building a Fairer Britain* (December 2010) states that equality matters because:

Failure to tackle discrimination and to provide equal opportunities, harms individuals, weakens our society and costs our economy. For example:

- *the National Audit Office estimated that the overall cost to the economy from failure to fully use the talents of people from ethnic minorities could be around £8.6 billion annually;*

- *the Women and Work Commission estimated the total potential benefits of increasing women's employment and tackling occupational gender segregation could be worth about £15 billion to £23 billion to the economy each year;*

- *the economic cost of violence against women in the UK is estimated to be £37.6 billion annually.*

At a time of global economic pressures, equality becomes more, not less, important. We are committed to tackling Britain's record deficit now, so that the next generation does not have to pay for the mistakes of this generation, and we will protect and safeguard those services that are crucial to individuals' life chances.

www.homeoffice.gov.uk/publications/equalities/equality-strategy-publications/equality-strategy/(accessed 11.09.11)

Your job role will give you the opportunity to tackle discrimination and raise awareness among your students.

To promote and advance equality and diversity effectively, it is important you understand some of the terminology used. In Appendix 4, you will find a glossary of terms which will prove a valuable starting point for your knowledge, and act as a useful reference.

Student differences

Student differences should be acknowledged, celebrated and embraced. All students should be included in the learning process and the learning environment should be suitable for everyone attending. Your teaching role requires you to be responsible for advancing equality and diversity in the learning environment. Advancing embeds equality and diversity at the heart of all aspects of teaching and learning and naturally takes into account students' needs. Advancing in this way should lead to improved outcomes for your students.

Examples of these differences are:

- ability
- accent and dialect
- age
- belief
- colour
- class
- clothing worn
- confidence
- criminal conviction
- culture
- disability – physical or mental
- domestic circumstances
- educational background
- employment status
- ethnic origin
- experience
- gender
- gender identity
- intelligence
- language
- learning difficulties
- marital status/civil partnership
- mental health
- nationality
- occupation
- parental status
- physical characteristics
- political conviction
- race
- religion
- sexual orientation
- social class or identity
- talent
- tradition
- transgender
- wealth

The benefits of promoting and advancing equality and diversity will help to ensure:

- a better understanding of religions, faiths and cultures within and across the group

- a climate of trust, respect and tolerance towards others

- a positive learning experience for all

- achievement of learning goals

- assessment is fair

- communication is open and honest

- students are content and happy

- diversity is recognised and celebrated

- effective teamwork

- improved working relationships

- motivation is increased

- individual needs are met

- resources are not discriminatory

- sessions can be planned to relate to all interests, abilities and cultures

- stereotyping, prejudice and discrimination are not demonstrated by you and are challenged when demonstrated by students

- open discussions are welcomed as an opportunity to challenge

Inclusive practice

An inclusive organisation will ensure students are not excluded for any legitimate reason, either directly or indirectly, from partaking in their chosen programme. All your students will bring with them valuable skills, knowledge and experiences. Try to draw on these and incorporate them within your sessions. Treat each of your students as an individual; each will have their own aspirations for their future and will be attending your sessions to help them get there. A quick way of including everyone is to welcome them as they enter, use their name whenever possible and use eye contact. If you notice anything untoward such as discrimination or bullying, you must deal with it immediately. If you use group activities, make sure all your students feel comfortable with who they are working with. You might need to allocate your students into groups rather than letting them choose their friends all the time. This will give them the opportunity to work with others.

Example

Ninghong commenced a Customer Service programme at the same time as 15 other students. Her English is quite good, but she always sat on her own and didn't want to work in a group. Her teacher asked her during the lunch break if anything was wrong. She confided she felt the others were making fun of her name and culture, but didn't want to make a formal complaint. Her teacher amended the next session to include greeting visitors from other countries, and used various activities to bring an awareness of other cultures to the group. The group were not aware this was a direct result of Ninghong's chat with her teacher. Afterwards, Ninghong felt more included in the group, and several students were showing an interest and asking her for more information about her culture.

Teaching and learning cycle

The teaching and learning cycle is so called as it can start at any stage and keep on going. However, all stages must be addressed for teaching and learning to be effective. There are opportunities at each stage to advance equality and diversity.

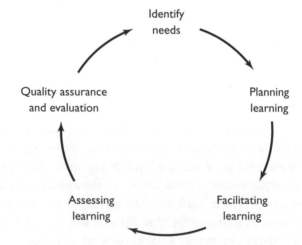

Figure 1.1 The teaching and learning cycle

The following table shows ways to promote inclusion and advance equality and diversity.

Identifying needs	Ascertaining students' specific and additional needs as well as their aspirations for the future.
	Ensuring all students can complete application and enrolment forms, for example using different languages or print sizes, electronic or hard copy.
	Ensuring interview notes are kept regarding any support requirements needed and these are communicated to relevant people, for example those with dyslexia, epilepsy, diabetes.
	Ensuring students have had access to impartial information, advice and guidance (IAG) to consider all their options.
	Ensuring programmes are offered at times everyone can attend.
	Exploring flexible programme delivery or blended learning approaches.
	Finding ways to overcome barriers such as finance, childcare, etc.
	Removing barriers to enable students to access information, staff, documents and buildings.
	Using initial assessment results to plan individual learning.
Planning learning	Ensuring a programme is in place that responds to the needs and aspirations of all students.
	Using appropriate and accessible resources.
	Agreeing individual learning plans/action plans.
	Creating resources and materials which positively promote all aspects of community and society, equality and diversity.
	Creating schemes of work and session plans to reflect how you will include all students in sessions.
	Differentiating your teaching approaches and activities to address individual differences, for example levels or speed of learning.
	Ensuring off-site visits are accessible by all, for example transport and stairs.
	Ensuring the environment is accessible to all students.
	Planning opportunities to develop motivation, self-esteem and confidence within your students.
	Planning your delivery to meet the needs of all learning styles.

Facilitating learning	Using a variety of teaching and learning approaches to suit all learning styles and student needs.
	Adapting resources as necessary.
	Avoiding favouritism and positive discrimination.
	Being approachable and accessible enabling your students to feel comfortable talking.
	Being aware that everyone has different experiences, interests, skills and knowledge which will affect their ability to develop and learn.
	Carrying out an icebreaker or energiser which includes everyone.
	Agreeing suitable ground rules.
	Challenging stereotyping, discrimination and prejudice as it happens.
	Drawing on personal experiences of students during each session.
	Embedding language, literacy, numeracy and ICT.
	Encouraging group discussions and activities where everyone can participate.
	Encouraging group work where students can mix and participate with all members of the group over a period of time.
	Encouraging respect and promoting understanding of student differences.
	Ensuring students have access to facilities, resources and equipment which is appropriate for the subject and level of learning.
	Ensuring the language and jargon you use is at an appropriate level.
	Following up absences and ensuring students have access to any missed material.
	Identifying where modifications or changes are needed to ensure everyone feels included.
	Involving all students within your session, using their name and asking individual questions.
	Not excluding any student for any reason.
	Providing a safe and supportive environment where everyone's contribution is valued.

Assessing learning	Adapting assessment activities where possible to meet any particular requirements or needs of students. Encouraging all students to reach their full potential. Ensuring assessment planning is individual and appropriate. Giving ongoing developmental feedback at a level to suit the student. Recognising and valuing individual achievements.
Quality assurance and evaluation	Communicating with your team members to ensure they are aware of any student requirements or issues. Evaluating your delivery to ensure you have included all students fully in your session. Liaising with the awarding organisation regarding any modifications required to the learning and assessment activities. Obtaining feedback from your students and others in different ways, for example verbally, written or electronically.

If you can develop the conditions for learning that are based on respect and trust and address the needs of individual students, you will have created an effective and inclusive teaching and learning environment.

Valuing equality and diversity

You should be positive and pro-active where equality and diversity are concerned, even if your own opinions differ from those of your students. You may have to challenge your own attitudes, values and beliefs. However, as a professional, you are first and foremost a teacher, and your personal opinions must not interfere with the teaching and learning process. You must also be careful not to indulge the minority, to the detriment of the majority.

If you ever feel unsure as to whether you, or other students and colleagues, are valuing equality and diversity, just ask yourself 'is this fair?', or, 'how would I feel in this situation?' or 'would I want to be treated in this way?' If your answer is a negative one, then make sure you do something about it. You may not always have the answer to this question especially where there is a difficulty in meeting the conflicting needs of students.

Example

A new student, Nadia, has arrived from Saudi Arabia and joined the group. She has been brought up to oppose homosexuality and her teacher, George, is aware there are two gay students in the group. During a group activity, George took the opportunity to explain that although people have different beliefs and views, they must not interfere with the learning process.

The changing and diverse nature of society poses many challenges for individuals, groups, employers and teachers. To demonstrate inclusion in its truest sense, equality, diversity and rights issues should be the norm. This will demonstrate to everyone that the issues do not only affect minority groups. The rights and needs of each person should be taken into account and not just the majority. The learning environment can be enriched through the diversity of the students and their experiences.

Those affected by stereotyping, prejudice and discrimination are not always in the minority. The Equality and Human Rights Commission's First Triennial Review *How Fair is Britain? Equality, Human Rights and Good Relations in 2010* states that across Britain, disabled adults are three times more likely than others to have no qualifications and women aged 40 earn on average 27 per cent less than men of the same age. Add to this the number of people who have been affected by prejudice and discrimination, for example due to their age, religion, gender or sexual orientation, and you can see that many individuals could be the subject of unfair treatment. This could be at some point in their lives, whether in education, employment or accessing goods and services. Having organisational policies, procedures and codes of practice, and following government legislation, will help you promote a more inclusive learning environment. You may like to access the following video link 'How fair is Britain' regarding the Review: www.equalityhumanrights.com/key-projects/how-fair-is-britain/video-overview/ (accessed 11.09.11).

Skills Funding Agency

The Skills Funding Agency (SFA) exists to make England better skilled and more competitive. Success for them is when:

> *Further Education efficiently meets the current and future needs of learners and employers; we offer comprehensive advice to learners, enabling them to make more informed choices; we improve access for employers to skills ensuring it is simplified, efficient and effective; we ensure that more people have the right skills that England needs to stay globally competitive.*

(skillsfundingagency.bis.gov.uk/aboutus/ [accessed 11.09.11])

You might be teaching students who are on programmes funded by the SFA and therefore will be able to contribute towards their *vision* by your own commitment to equality and diversity within your organisation.

Activity

Find out if you will be teaching on programmes funded by the SFA, or any other funding organisation, for example Young People's Learning Agency (YPLA). What are their commitments to equality and diversity? Will you be required to maintain any particular records or statistics? If so, why do you think that is?

Embedding equality and diversity

As a teacher, you need to ensure you are embedding all aspects of equality and diversity within the curriculum you are responsible for. You might be inspected at some time and will need to demonstrate how you are embedding aspects within your teaching.

A report by Her Majesty's Inspectorate (HMI) *Race equality in further education* found:

> *The promotion of equality and diversity through the curriculum is a common feature, but it is rarely embedded consistently across the whole curriculum.*

(2005: 3)

An example of promoting and advancing equality could start with the way your organisation advertises their programmes, to ensure they are promoting accessibility for all prospective students. This would then follow through the recruitment and interviewing stages, induction, initial assessment, teaching, assessment and evaluation. Examples of demonstrating inclusion throughout these stages could be by the use of pictures in marketing materials of students from different ethnic backgrounds and those with visible and invisible disabilities.

When teaching, always include your students in relevant activities during sessions, and throughout the full learning process, rather than excluding anyone for any reason. The best way to ensure you are effectively including all students, and treating them equally, is to ask them what they need. If asked, students will usually tell you what their needs are, whether that is from a religious or cultural point of view, or if they have a particular need in terms of a disability or otherwise. However, it's difficult to help your students if they don't tell you about any specific issues, needs or concerns they might have. You could ask if there is anything you could do to help make their learning experience a more positive one and ascertain what they *can do* rather than what they *can't do*. However, anything you do would have to be reasonable, and not seen as favouritism by other students. Encouraging them to tell you when you are on your own at an appropriate time would save your student any embarrassment they might feel when in front of their peers.

To value and promote diversity among your students, you need to embrace their differences, encourage interaction and support, and challenge any negative beliefs either held by yourself or demonstrated by other students.

The Government's Home Office *Equality Strategy – Building a Fairer Britain* (December 2010) states:

> *Equality is not an add-on, but an integral part of this government's commitment to build a stronger economy and fairer society. This strategy sets out a new approach to delivering equality: one that moves away from treating people as groups or 'equality strands' and instead recognises that we are a nation of 62 million individuals.*

> (www.homeoffice.gov.uk/publications/equalities/equality-strategy-publications/equality-strategy/ (accessed 17.10.11))

Always treat your students and colleagues fairly, with dignity and respect, not just as you would wish to be treated. Try to become familiar with the specific customs or needs that a student's faith or culture might require. This will ensure you are advancing equality and diversity as part of your everyday teaching, and including rather than excluding students for any reason.

Activity

Do you feel you have excluded anyone you work with, or a student, intentionally or not? Think about how you conduct yourself in the staff room at break times, how you communicate with your colleagues and students, and the types of resources you use when teaching. Do you have a positive attitude or do you feel you have been influenced by others?

It could be that you follow what other people do, rather than making your own decisions regarding your attitudes, values and beliefs. When teaching, you should build up a climate of trust, openness and honesty with your colleagues and students, and encourage them to integrate and treat each other with respect. Students should be supported to achieve their maximum potential without making them feel excluded or discriminated against, for example needing time to attend a religious or cultural event. Initial assessment will help you obtain any specific information regarding individual students that may need to be addressed. However, if you are not involved in this process, or it doesn't take place, make sure you talk to each of your students to find out if they have any particular needs.

Knowledge of dates of relevant religious festivals or other events that may impact upon your teaching sessions and students' attendance will help when planning your scheme of work. Legislation does not determine when holidays must be taken, and nobody is entitled to more holiday than others because of their religion or ethnic origin. However, some religious festivals will require students to be absent from learning as they attend certain events either at a place of worship or with their families. Discussion with students around these events is vital and you may authorise their absence in line with the policies of your organisation.

Example

Fatima is due to fast as part of Ramadan and will not be eating or drinking during daylight hours. She explained to her teacher beforehand that she may feel tired and find it difficult to concentrate during sessions. Her teacher was understanding and told her she could leave the room if she wished. Her teacher also offered to e-mail Fatima the work that she would miss and to have a tutorial after Ramadan to go through it with her.

The Excellence Gateway has a wealth of resources and information regarding equality and diversity. If you get the opportunity have a look at their website www.excellencegateway.org.uk and carry out a search for Equality and Diversity.

Extension Activity

What do the following terms mean to you in your teaching role: equality, diversity, inequality and discrimination? Explain how inequality and discrimination can impact upon individuals, communities and society.

The Equality Act (2010)

The Equality Act (2010) replaced all previous anti-discrimination legislation and consolidated it into a single act for England, Scotland and Wales (there are separate requirements in Northern Ireland). It provides rights for people not to be directly discriminated against or harassed because they have an *association* with a disabled person, nor must people be directly discriminated against or harassed because they are wrongly *perceived* as disabled. Reasonable adjustments must take place during teaching and learning activities to lessen or remove the effects of a disadvantage to a student with a disability.

The Equality Act (2010) has three main aims:

- to simplify, streamline and harmonise the law;

- to strengthen the law;

- to support progress in promoting equality and achieving year on year improved outcomes.

> *Over the last 40 years, more than 20 pieces of equality legislation have been introduced, with over 2,500 pages of guidance. This legislation has developed incrementally, leading to gaps, complexity and inconsistency. Yet despite this plethora of legislation, persistent inequalities remain. For example, disabled people are twice as likely to be unemployed, and at the current rate it will take 100 years for people from black and minority ethnic backgrounds to have the same job prospects as white people. Children eligible for free school meals, a proxy indicator of poverty or social disadvantage, do significantly less well than other children at school at every stage; only 14% of these young people progress to higher education, for example, compared with 33% of their peers.*

(LSIS, 2011: 3)

Protected characteristics

The Act identifies nine *protected characteristics*, changes the definitions of discrimination and places a new extended Public Sector Equality Duty on public bodies, with two new specific duties: to harmonise and extend the role of positive action and restrict the use of health and disability-related questions during recruitment and selection, and strengthen the powers of employment tribunals.

A protected characteristic refers to aspects of a person's identity which are explicitly protected from discrimination.

They are:

- age
- disability
- gender
- gender identity
- marriage and civil partnership
- maternity and pregnancy
- race
- religion and belief
- sexual orientation

All nine protected characteristics are covered in the employment duties of the Act. However, the protected characteristic of marriage and civil partnerships is not included in the education duties of the Act.

Examples of the protected characteristics are:

- *age*: older people, younger people
- *disability*: physical or sensory impairments, mental health difficulties, long-term medical conditions, learning difficulties, neuro diverse conditions such as dyslexia, autism, tourettes or attention deficit hyperactivity disorder (ADHD); for an impairment to be a disability, its effect on normal day-to-day activities must be substantial – the Equality Act (2010) now defines substantial to mean *more than minor or trivial*
- *gender*: male, female
- *gender identity*: transsexual people, transgender people, men and women with transsexual history
- *marriage and civil partnership*: married people, people in a civil partnership, single people
- *maternity and pregnancy*: pregnant women, people on maternity leave, women who have recently given birth

- *race*: nationality, ethnic background, origin or heritage

- *religion and belief*: people from different faith groups, people with a philosophical belief, people with no religion or belief

- *sexual orientation*: gay and lesbian people, bisexual people, heterosexual/ straight people

When preparing your teaching materials and resources, you should ensure you use representations of people with protected characteristics as well as those without.

The term *advance*

The term *promote* was previously used in discrimination legislation, this has been replaced with the word *advance* – the intention being to move forward, to get somewhere and to achieve improved outcomes for your students.

Advance involves organisations having due regard to:

- removing/minimising disadvantages experienced by students who share a protected characteristic that are connected to that characteristic

- taking steps to meet the needs of students who share a relevant protected characteristic that are different from the needs of students who don't share it

- encouraging students with a relevant protected characteristic to fully participate in activities where participation is disproportionately low

The Act recognises the following types of discrimination which will be covered throughout the chapters of this book:

- direct discrimination, including association and perception discrimination

- indirect discrimination

- harassment

- victimisation

- discrimination arising from a disability

- failure to make reasonable adjustments

Public sector duties to promote race, disability and gender equality are replaced and extended in the Act by a new Public Sector Equality Duty which will require organisations to give due regard to:

- eliminate discrimination, harassment and victimisation

- advance equality of opportunity

- foster good relations

The public sector duty covers eight of the nine protected characteristics of the Act: age, disability, gender, gender identity, pregnancy and maternity, race, religion and belief, sexual orientation. Only the first aim of the duty, *to eliminate discrimination, harassment and victimisation* will apply to the ninth protected characteristic of marriage and civil partnerships.

Types of discrimination

Under the Equality Act (2010), there are seven different *types of discrimination*.

1. Associative discrimination: direct discrimination against someone because they are associated with another person with a protected characteristic. For example, Mary receives verbal abuse because she is friends with a transsexual student.

2. Direct discrimination: discrimination because of a protected characteristic. For example, Terry, aged 59, was not offered a place on a Motor Vehicle Maintenance programme as the teacher felt he was too old. The rest of the group were under 30.

3. Indirect discrimination: when a rule or policy which applies to everyone can disadvantage a person with a protected characteristic. For example, Aara wears a burqa and is working towards a Certificate in Hotel Reception at college. Part of the programme involves a week at a work placement. The local hotel refused her a place as they said their guests preferred to see receptionists' faces.

4. Discrimination by perception: direct discrimination against someone because others think they have a protected characteristic. For example, George was taunted because he stammered, even though his stammer was not a disability.

5. Harassment: behaviour deemed offensive by the recipient. For example, Joseph has been following Marla home from her day release classes. Yesterday he said that if she didn't go out with him, he would spread a rumour that she was gay.

6. Harassment by a third party: the harassment of staff or others by people not directly employed by an organisation, such as an external

consultant or visitor. For example, the training organisation is having a new roof installed. The contractors whistle at the female students as they walk by and make sexual remarks.

7. Victimisation: discrimination against someone because they made or supported a complaint under equality legislation. For example, Abha, a white student, saw a black student subjected to racially abusive language in the canteen. She complained that this has caused her environment to be offensive. Next time she went into the canteen, she was also subjected to abusive language.

The Equality Act is explored further throughout the chapters of this book and the protected characteristics are detailed in Chapter 6.

Extension Activity

Search the internet for the Equality Act (2010). Find out as much information as you can about how it impacts upon education. Give a different example of an instance that could occur for each of the seven different types of discrimination, and how you would deal with each occurrence.

Promoting a positive culture

Promoting a positive culture should occur throughout the whole student journey, i.e. from before they commence to after they leave. The way your programmes are advertised, how your organisation recruits students, the language used in promotional materials and access to buildings and facilities all play a part in this.

When your students start with you, you should carry out an appropriate icebreaker and then agree some ground rules. This will help set the scene for what is acceptable and unacceptable behaviour.

Icebreakers

Students can be quiet, shy, nervous or apprehensive when they first commence. Carrying out an icebreaker is a good way of everyone getting to know each other's name and encouraging communication to take place. It will encourage your students to relax, and give them confidence to speak or ask questions in front of others.

Icebreakers can be quite simple, for example asking your students to introduce themselves in front of the group. However, this can be intimidating if none of the students have met before. A way round this is to form the group into pairs and ask them to talk to each other for five minutes about their hobbies, interests and reason for being there. They may find they have something in common and create a bond. You can then ask each person to introduce the person they have been talking to. People may not feel comfortable talking about themselves to a group of strangers, so another person introducing them takes this anxiety away. A good idea is to note down your students' names when they introduce each other, on a rough sketch of a seating plan. This will help you remember their names as it's likely they will return to the same position at the next session. You could also note something personal about them which you could use in a future conversation. This shows that you are taking an interest in each student.

Always introduce yourself first otherwise students may be wondering what your name is, or whether you are their permanent teacher or just someone facilitating the icebreaker. First impressions count; therefore you need to portray that you are a professional, knowledgeable teacher who is competent and approachable.

More complex icebreakers can involve games or activities, known as energisers, but the outcome should be for your students to relax, enjoy the activity, communicate and ascertain each other's names. Icebreakers help retain attention, keep motivation high and help the group to work together. All students should be included and you should manage the activity carefully to ensure everyone can actively take part. You may wish to include yourself in the icebreaker, or just observe what is happening. If you include yourself, don't get too personal, resist the temptation to be everyone's *friend* and remain professional throughout.

Whichever way you use an icebreaker or an energiser, it should be designed to be a fun and light-hearted activity to:

- break down barriers
- build confidence
- create a suitable learning environment
- enable students to talk confidently in front of their peers
- encourage communication, motivation, interaction, teamwork and inclusion
- establish trust

CORNWALL COLLEGE
LEARNING CENTRE

- get the programme off to a good start
- help students relax
- introduce students to each other
- reduce apprehension and nervousness
- reduce intimidation

Activity

Imagine you have a new group of 15 students starting next week who have never met each other before. What sort of icebreaker would you carry out with them and why?

Your organisation may have icebreakers for you to use or you could design your own or search the internet for ideas. Keep your icebreaker short and simple and always evaluate how it went to enable you to modify or improve it for the future.

Ground rules

Ground rules are boundaries, rules and conditions within which students can safely work and learn. They should underpin appropriate behaviour and respect for everyone in the group, including the teacher, and ensure the session runs smoothly. If they are not set, problems may occur which could disrupt the session and lead to misunderstandings. It is best to agree the ground rules during the first session, perhaps after the icebreaker once everyone is feeling more relaxed.

Ground rules should always be discussed and negotiated with your students rather than imposed upon them. Using an activity to do this will help students feel included, take ownership of, and hopefully follow them. Some ground rules might be renegotiated or added to throughout the programme, for example changing the break time. Others might not be negotiable but imposed, for example health and safety requirements.

Example

- *arriving on time and returning from breaks punctually*
- *no anti-social behaviour, offensive language or swearing*

- *respecting others' views and beliefs*
- *following health and safety regulations*
- *handing in work on time*
- *paying attention and fully participating*
- *switching off mobile phones and electronic devices*
- *leaving the area tidy*

Whatever method you use to agree these, make sure they are not open to any misinterpretation.

If your students attend sessions taken by other teachers, it is a good idea to discuss with them what your group has agreed, to ensure consistency. You might also take your students for other subjects and therefore have a core list of ground rules for all sessions, with some specific ones for each particular subject.

If you can lead by example you will help create a culture of mutual compliance which should lead to effective teaching and learning taking place.

Creating an inclusive culture

As a professional teacher in a diverse and multicultural society, you need to help promote and advance a positive and inclusive culture within your teaching and learning environment. Think of culture as *the way of life,* or *the way things are done* within your organisation. It's the beliefs and customs of a particular group of people, for example those you work with. If you feel your organisation isn't very proactive in promoting and advancing a positive culture, there's no reason to be complacent; you can do things yourself to ensure your students are all treated fairly. You may need to challenge your own attitudes, values and beliefs, to accept and respect others. If other people see your positive attitude and the proactive ways you embrace equality and diversity with your students, this may help improve the culture of your organisation. If you are working towards the teaching standards, you will need to:

> Establish a purposeful learning environment where learners feel safe, secure, confident and valued. (BP1.1)

> Establish and maintain procedures with learners which promote and maintain appropriate behaviour, communication and respect for others, while challenging discriminatory behaviour and attitudes. (BP1.2)

(LLUK, 2007: 5)

To help achieve this, and to ensure your students have an equal and fair chance to improve their education, you need to recognise that people are different. This can be the way they look, behave, dress, their beliefs, and/or where they live and work, their background, culture, gender, age, etc. In a diverse and multicultural society, recognising and accepting individual differences is part of embracing equality and diversity.

Activity

Make a list of what makes you different, and what makes you the same as a colleague, friend or family member. You probably found your different list was longer than your same list. This is a simple activity to demonstrate diversity and difference. You might like to carry out the activity with your students, asking them what makes them different to the person sitting next to them. You can then discuss how important it is to accept people for what they are, and to put aside personal opinions.

Sometimes, assumptions are made about people because of how they look or act. This might be deliberate on their part to *fit in* with a particular group, for fear of discrimination or being left out. As a teacher, you need to get to know your students as individuals, to encourage them to be *themselves* and to promote an inclusive culture within your group. This can lead to greater confidence and a sense of belonging on the students' part, better communication within the group, and respect for individual differences.

Students may have attitudes, values and beliefs which they have inherited from others, without having the opportunity to develop their own. These could include set ways of thinking, or preconceived ideas of other cultures that are not based on fact. Ignorance should be no excuse for treating someone unfairly. Part of your role should be to encourage a climate of acceptance and support, informed by fact and not based upon a person's background, upbringing, culture or religion, etc. Your students need to accept they may have different attitudes, values and beliefs to other students, but that these should not interfere with the group cohesion or learning process. Indeed, you may feel differently about certain issues, and you don't have to necessarily believe or agree with all your students, but you must not let your opinions interfere with the teaching and learning process. You must also be careful not to be biased in any way towards a particular type of group or individual.

To ensure an inclusive culture and access to all, your organisation could have the following:

- adjustable desks

- automatic doors

- external ramps

- facilities to meet dietary needs

- handouts: enlarged text, different fonts, coloured paper

- internal ramps

- lifts

- loop/minicom systems

- resources which can also be accessed electronically

- support workers

- tape/digital recorders

- toilets on all floors

- wide doors

Creating an inclusive environment

To create an inclusive environment, you should involve all your students during your sessions in a way they feel able to respond, and not exclude anyone for any reason, either directly or indirectly. Asking each student a question, rather than focusing on those you know will have the answer, is a way of including everyone. To make sure you do ask everyone a question, you could keep a list of their names and tick these off as you go along to ensure you don't miss anyone out. All students have the right to be valued as individuals, and are entitled to attend and participate in their chosen programme and to feel safe. You should always differentiate your approach and resources to meet any individual needs.

A curriculum offer should have something for everyone and be as inclusive as possible in order to ensure that as wide a range of learners as possible can take advantage of it ... A curriculum for diversity should encompass everything that a provider has to offer, including what is taught, who teaches it, what is known and expected of learners, as well as where learning takes place. It is a perspective on adult education that should permeate everything.

(White and Weaver, 2007: ix)

You might not be in a position to design various aspects of the curriculum, but you are responsible for the groups and/or individuals you teach, and the experiences they have while they are with you. To help benefit your students, you need to familiarise yourself with the diverse nature of today's society, race, religions and cultures to be able to offer equal experiences to all your students.

Activity

Compare and contrast four beliefs, faiths and/or religions in our society. (For example, Agnostic, Atheist, Buddhist, Christian, Hinduism, Islam, Jehovah's Witness, Judaism, Mormon, Pagan, Rastafari, Shinto, Sikhism, Taoism, etc.) Having some knowledge of these will help you understand and appreciate the diverse nature of others.

Becoming knowledgeable about aspects such as beliefs, faiths and religions will help you appreciate your students' various backgrounds and differences. Embracing their differences whenever possible will help include your students and enable them to be more confident, feel safe and have a sense of belonging. Naturally occurring opportunities might arise for you to incorporate and embed these differences. For example, discussing current and relevant news stories or situations in television programmes and dramas. You could also create themes throughout the year to celebrate events such as Chinese New Year, Diwali, Eed, etc.

People naturally have perceptions about others, which can often be wrong; therefore information and knowledge can help change how your students perceive each other. There are many individual and social factors that should be taken into consideration. These can encompass: physical, mental and emotional characteristics; likes and dislikes; attitudes, values and beliefs; personality traits; politics, morals and ethics; type of household; social identity; clothing worn; and past experiences.

The Centre for Excellence in Leadership states:

People are diverse in the way they learn. Learning approaches may be inherent, but may also be shaped by cultural experience. The greater the variety of experiences a learning group may have at its disposal, the greater the capacity for thinking differently and problem-solving in innovative ways. There are a high number of learners from minority groups in the learning and skills sector. For providers, there are challenges in engaging those learners and keeping them on track and this is exacerbated by issues such as institutional discrimination. An organisational culture which encourages diversity and provides culturally relevant role models creates a more representative learning environment, and leads to better results.

(2005: 5)

Hopefully, your organisation will embrace the above statement, and you are working within a culture which promotes and adopts positive learning approaches. If not, you may need to encourage change, within yourself, and your students and colleagues, as a start.

Attitudes

Attitudes towards equality have changed in recent years. As little as half a century ago, sexism, racism and other forms of prejudice spread through almost every aspect of daily life. Today, we live in a society where prejudice and discrimination are illegal, and are almost always socially unacceptable. We are more tolerant of difference, and less tolerant of discrimination. The way we talk about ourselves, our values and the standards of conduct that we expect all suggest that we aspire to be a fair society, free from discrimination.

These changes have made a meaningful difference in the lives of many people who may be subject to disadvantage because of who or what they are. More importantly they have transformed the expectations of most British people about what constitutes reasonable behaviour and what a decent society should look like. However, what happens in the real world can be a very different experience, from the harassment of disabled people, to homophobic bullying, to stereotypes that prevent older people from giving their best in the workplace. Society is not as fair as it could be and inequalities are sometimes ignored for fear of recrimination from peer groups. To make progress towards being a fairer society, you should take opportunities to discuss issues with your students whenever possible.

Having a positive attitude in front of others, ensuring all students are included in activities, and encouraging a professional working relationship between everyone will help promote an understanding and tolerant climate during your sessions. If your students and colleagues see your positive and proactive attitude, it will help them adopt the same, therefore having an impact on changing the culture and inequality.

To ensure equality and diversity is no longer viewed as something only affecting minority groups, any issues need to be viewed not as issues, but something to be *explored* and *celebrated*. Students could be personally affected by stereotyping, prejudice and/or discrimination when attending sessions, for example a disability could result in non-attendance or non-achievement. As a teacher, you need to ensure all your students value each other and that the basic rights they are entitled to, for example to learn in a comfortable and safe environment, are met.

Policies

When you started at your organisation, your induction should have included details of all policies, including equality and diversity. Other policies you should be aware of include:

- access

- appeals

- complaints

- confidentiality of information

- copyright and data protection

- fair assessment

- health and safety

You should also bring these to the attention of your students, perhaps during their initial interview or induction session. However, having a policy is not enough; there should be a *working group* or *committee* to ensure they are promoted, monitored and regularly reviewed. The content of the policy should be practised by both staff and students.

Example

The organisation fully supports all principles of equality and diversity, and opposes any unfair or unlawful discrimination on the grounds of ability, age, colour, culture, disability, domestic circumstances, employment status, ethnic origin, gender, gender reassignment, learning difficulties, marital status/civil partnership, nationality, political conviction, race, religion or belief, sexual orientation and/or social background.

The organisation aims to ensure that equality and diversity are promoted and advanced among all staff and students, and that unfair or unlawful discrimination, whether direct or indirect, is eliminated to promote a climate of equality and respect. All staff and learners can expect to work in an environment free from harassment and bullying.

Combined together, equality and diversity will drive your organisation to comply with anti-discrimination legislation, as well as emphasising the positive benefits. This includes embracing student experiences, cultures and differences, while enabling each individual's maximum potential to be fulfilled.

People are disabled by their environment – the attitudes of others and the policies, practices and procedures of organisations.

(www.worldofinclusion.com/inclusion_education.htm (accessed 06.08.11))

If you feel the learning environment at your organisation, and the policies, practices and procedures are hindering your students' learning, you must talk to the person responsible for equality and diversity.

Your organisation should also have a commitment to disabled people by having a Disability Equality Scheme.

Example

The organisation will work to reduce disadvantages, discrimination and inequalities of opportunity. We will advance equality and diversity for our students, staff, the community and stakeholders. We will focus on increased independence, choices and involvement in decision making as well as removing any barriers to access and making reasonable adjustments where necessary.

Ways to advance the commitment include:

● continuing to affirm a culture where students and staff feel able to declare their disability so that reasonable adjustments can be made

● enabling a culture where harassment and discrimination is unacceptable

● encouraging applications from disabled people and ensuring that the application, short-listing and interviewing process gives them equality of opportunity

- involving disabled people in evaluating the services offered

- offering training to students and staff in disability awareness

- promoting positive attitudes towards disabled people through advertising materials, notices, programme resources, the intranet and website

- providing a forum for disabled students to voice their concerns

- training staff to have the skills to take positive action when necessary

- working with disabled people and relevant organisations to achieve equality of opportunity

Equality analysis

All policies should be regularly reviewed and have an action plan to ensure the requirements are being met. Feedback should be obtained from students and staff to ensure this has been put into practice. An *Equality Impact Assessment*, now known as an *Equality Analysis* due to the Equality Act (2010), should be carried out to assess how the services are provided to disabled people and what impact they have had. The terminology has altered to reflect a change in emphasis; the intention is for organisations to focus more attention on properly analysing the effects of equality and diversity on existing or new policy and practice, and less attention on completing a document, which can be an end in itself. However, collecting and distributing information is not the end. Information should be analysed and used to eliminate discrimination, advance equality and foster good relations. If you are involved with preparing an equality analysis, ensure you concentrate on collecting and analysing information that matters, not what is easily available, and try to find a balance regarding the amount of information you produce. You must meet the requirements of the Data Protection Act (1998) and the Gender Recognition Act (2004) when publishing your information.

The results of the analysis should be given to all staff and could be made available to the public perhaps on your organisation's intranet and website. The document should highlight areas for improvement and lead to an action plan with clear objectives.

When creating an action plan, you should set objectives and consider:

- all aims and protected characteristics of the Equality Act (2010)

- all functions and activities, for example service delivery and staff recruitment

- equality information

- equality analysis, including details of information considered when carrying out analysis

- engagement activities

Engagement is a broad term to cover all consultation and involvement activities in the context of equality. Objectives should be appropriate and focus on the most pressing equality gaps. Organisations should also set out how progress will be measured and reported.

Research conducted by Dr Christine Rose (2009) on behalf of the Equality and Human Rights Commission explored practice in the public sector in setting equality objectives.

Some of the key messages were to:

- Develop a sound evidence base before identifying, devising and prioritising equality objectives. This ensures an organisation focuses on genuine issues within its own context.

- Ensure evidence includes qualitative and quantitative information, for workforce and service delivery.

- Provide transparency and clarity about the outcomes of information gathering activities to demonstrate publicly the reasons for choosing objectives.

- Consider how to capture the voice identified, for example people with mental health difficulties, gypsies and travellers, and people with learning difficulties, caring responsibilities or on a low income.

- Avoid equality objectives that are little more than overarching aims, top-level commitments, or maintenance of current practice. Instead, devise specific objectives that clearly demonstrate how successful implementation might lead to tangible and measurable improvements in equality.

- Prioritise objectives to focus on the most significant issues for the organisation's remit. Ensure people who have participated in consultation activities have an opportunity to refine equality objectives.

- Recognise that successful engagement is transparent and influential; this means making clear to all who participated in engagement activities how people's views influenced the choice of objectives, and how people have been involved in early and final decisions on setting and prioritising equality objectives.

- Cross-reference each equality objective with the aim or aims of the Equality Duty that the objective is attempting to meet. This ensures that all aspects of the duty have been considered.

- Evidence the link between the equality objective and the organisation's strategic or corporate objectives.

Activity

Locate the equality and diversity policy within your organisation. When is it due for review and who is responsible for it? Would you recommend any changes, or do you feel it is acceptable? Obtain and read your organisation's most recent Equality Impact Assessment or Equality Analysis.

If you had difficulty locating the policy, your students may also have difficulty. It could be that it's called something else, for example an *Equal Opportunities Policy*. Having looked at it, would you know what to do if you, or a student, had a problem, or do you feel you would like to be a part of the working group or committee? Usually, a policy will be accompanied by a procedure that may be located elsewhere. This will state the process that should be gone through if there was a problem or complaint, and what will be done about it, within specific timeframes.

To help promote and advance equality and diversity, organisations should ensure:

- a wide range of relevant services are available to support learning

- awareness is raised through relevant training

- barriers to participation are removed

- equality and diversity is reflected in the safer recruitment and selection of staff and students

- problems and complaints are followed up by the working group or committee

- staff and students are supported as necessary

- staff are aware of the diverse nature of today's society

- staff are familiar with current legislation

- the teaching environment and resources are appropriate, fair and inclusive

- there is a current and relevant policy which is promoted, monitored and regularly reviewed

The policy should be monitored on an ongoing basis, for example gathering information and data to support any problems or complaints, ensuring there is no unintentional discrimination, and keeping track of recruitment, training and development. The policy should also be reviewed in the light of any legislative changes or organisational amendments. If your organisation makes a decision to amend a policy or introduce a new policy, an equality impact assessment should be conducted to identify whether or not the proposed policy changes will have a detrimental impact on anyone in the organisation. Having a policy often leads to a *reactive* situation, where problems are dealt with afterwards. However, it's best to be *proactive* and avoid problems occurring in the first place. Policies should be designed to prevent events or problems, whereas a procedure will be *reactive* and carried out after an event or problem has occurred.

Example

Binder's college is hoping to recruit another female to the computing department; there are currently seven males and only one female. The senior management think that, to address the balance of males and females, they will be exempt from legislation. They ask the equality and diversity working group to look at their advertisement. The group advises that it is illegal to advertise purely for a female.

It is not acceptable to discriminate in favour of a particular group, for example, females. In this example, the senior management should look at their recruitment and selection procedures to ensure that they are not discriminating and will employ the right person for the job. The law does allow for organisations to *encourage* *applications* from under-represented groups, but does not allow for *selection* to be made simply on the basis of race or sex. The only time that you can discriminate in favour of a particular sex is if it is a genuine occupational qualification (GOQ) for a particular job, for example if the job is restricted to one sex as it requires living in single sex accommodation, or is in a single sex establishment.

Safeguarding

Safeguarding is a term used to refer to the duties and responsibilities that those providing a health, social or education service have to perform to protect individuals and vulnerable people from harm. Following the publication of the Safeguarding Vulnerable Groups Act in 2006, a vetting and barring scheme was established in autumn 2008. This Act created an

Independent Barring Board to take all discretionary decisions on whether individuals should be barred from working with children and/or vulnerable adults. You will be bound by this Act if you work with children (those under the age of 18 years in training) and/or vulnerable adults. You will need to attend Safeguarding training every three years (for some staff every two years depending upon their Safeguarding involvement).

A vulnerable adult is defined as a person aged 18 years or over, who is in receipt of or may be in need of community care services by reason of 'mental or other disability, age or illness and who is or may be unable to take care of him or herself, or unable to protect him or herself against significant harm or exploitation'.

(Bonnerjea, 2009: 9)

This could be anyone needing formal help to live in society, for example a young mother, someone with a learning disability or a recently released prisoner. If your organisation is inspected by Ofsted, they will be asking your students how safe they feel and whether they are able to give you feedback regarding any concerns they may have.

You have a duty of care and a personal responsibility towards all your students and should apply six key elements of appropriate service provision:

- choice
- confidentiality
- dignity
- independence
- individuality
- respect

There are four key processes that should be followed to ensure your students are safe:

1. an assessment of their needs
2. planning services to meet these needs
3. intervention if necessary when you have a concern
4. reviewing the services offered

If you have any concerns regarding a student, for example if you feel they are being bullied or may be at risk of harm or abuse, you must refer to your organisation's Designated Safeguarding Officer (DSO) immediately. It would be useful to find out who this person is if you don't already know. Never be tempted to get personally involved with your student's situation, always refer them to a specialist.

Every local authority will have a Local Safeguarding Children Board (LSCB). LSCBs are responsible for local arrangements for protecting children and young people. If you have any concerns relating to anyone who holds a position of trust or responsibility for children or young people, you should report them to the Local Authority Designated Officer (LADO).

Extension Activity

Make a list of your strengths and areas for development regarding promoting equality, valuing diversity and safeguarding students. Take into account feedback from students, perhaps from a recent evaluation activity, and from colleagues, perhaps from peer assessments or appraisals. What can you do to address your identified areas for development?

Summary

In this chapter you have learnt about:

- meanings and benefits of equality and diversity
- the Equality Act (2010)
- promoting a positive culture

Cross-referencing grid

This chapter contributes towards the following: scope (S), knowledge (K) and practice (P) aspects of the Professional Teaching Standards (A–F domains) and the Equality and Diversity assessment criteria at levels 3 and 4. Full details of the learning outcomes and assessment criteria for the units can be found in the appendices.

Domain	Standards
A	AS1, AS2, AS3, AS4, AS5, AS6, AS7
	AK1.1, AK2.1, AK2.2, AK3.1, AK4.2, AK5.1, AK5.2, AK6.1, AK6.2
	AP1.1, AP2.1, AP2.2, AP3.1, AP5.1, AP5.2, AP6.1, AP6.2, AP7.1
B	BS1, BS2, BS3, BS4
	BK1.1, BK1.2, BK1.3, BK2.2, BK2.5, BK3.4
	BP1.1, BP1.2, BP2.5
C	
D	DS1, DK1.1, DP1.1, DP1.3
E	
F	FS1, FS2, FK1.1, FK1.2, FK4.1, FK4.2, FP1.2, FP4.1
Equality and Diversity unit	Assessment criteria
Level 3	1.1, 1.2, 1.3, 2.1, 2.2, 2.3, 3.2, 3.3, 4.1, 4.2
Level 4	1.1, 1.2, 1.3, 2.1, 2.2, 2.3, 3.2, 3.3, 4.1, 4.2

Theory focus

References and further information

Bonnerjea, L (2009) *Safeguarding Adults Report on the consultation on the review of 'No Secrets'*. London: Department of Health

CEL (2005) *Leading Change in Equality and Diversity – The Centre for Excellence in Leadership's Strategy for Improving Diversity in Leadership in the Learning and Skills Sector*. London: CEL

Daniels, K and MacDonald, L (2005) *Equality, Diversity and Discrimination*. London: Chartered Institute of Personnel and Development

Department for Education and Skills (DfES) (2006) *Safeguarding Children and Safer Recruitment in Education*. London: DfES

DTI (2006) *Work and Families: Choice and Flexibility*. London: Department of Trade and Industry, 06/707

Her Majesty's Inspectorate (2005) *Race equality in further education*. London: HMI

HMI Report (2005) *Race Equality in Further Education: Progress and good practice in colleges in the further education sector*. London: HMI 2463

HMI (2006) *Working Together to Safeguard Children: A guide to inter-agency working to safeguard and promote the welfare of children*. London: HM Government

Home Office (2010) *The Equality Strategy – Building a Fairer Britain*. London: Home Office

Learning and Skills Council (2007) *Equality and Diversity – What's that then?* East Midlands LSC

LLUK (2007) *New Overarching Professional Teaching Standards*. London: LLUK

LSIS (2011) *New Equality Act 2010*. Coventry: Learning and Skills Improvement Service

Press for Change (2007) *Guidance on trans equality in post school education*. London: Unison

Rose, C (2009) Final report to the Equality and Human Rights Commission

Spencer, L (2005) *Diversity Pocketbook*. Alresford: Management Pocketbooks Ltd

White, L and Weaver, S (2007) *Curriculum for Diversity Guide*. Leicester: NIACE

Websites

Data Protection Act (2003) – http://regulatorylaw.co.uk/Data_Protection.html

Disability Equality in Education – www.worldofinclusion.com/inclusion_education.htm

Employment Tribunals Online – www.employmenttribunals.gov.uk

Equality Act (2010) – www.legislation.gov.uk/ukpga/2010/15/contents

Equality and Diversity Forum – www.edf.org.uk

Equality and Human Rights Commission – www.equalityhumanrights.com

Equality for Lesbians, Gay Men and Bisexuals – www.stonewall.org.uk

Excellence Gateway – www.excellencegateway.org.uk

Freedom of Information Act (2000) – www.opsi.gov.uk/Acts/acts2000/ukpga_20000036_en_1

Gender Recognition Act (2004) – www.legislation.gov.uk/ukpga/2004/7/contents

Health and Safety Executive – www.hse.gov.uk

Home Office Equality Strategy – www.homeoffice.gov.uk/publications/equalities/equality-strategy-publications/equality-strategy/

Icebreakers – http://adulted.about.com/od/icebreakers/Ice_Breakers.htm

Immigration Advice Service – www.iasservices.org.uk

Mental health – www.mind.org.uk

Skills Funding Agency – http://skillsfundingagency.bis.gov.uk

Working together to safeguard children – www.workingtogetheronline.co.uk/

Workplace Bullying – www.workplacebullying.co.uk

Young People's Learning Agency – www.ypla.gov.uk

2 ADVANCING EQUALITY AND VALUING DIVERSITY

Introduction

In this chapter you will learn about:

- applying the principles of equality and diversity
- advancing equality
- benefits of diversity

There are activities and examples which will help you reflect on the above and assist your understanding of how to advance equality and value diversity. At the end of each section is an extension activity to stretch and challenge your learning further.

At the end of the chapter, there is a cross-referencing grid showing how the content of this chapter contributes towards the Professional Teaching Standards and the Equality and Diversity assessment criteria at levels 3 and 4. There is also a theory focus with relevant references, further information and websites you might like to refer to.

Applying the principles of equality and diversity

When applying and advancing the principles of equality and diversity in your teaching practice there are many legal, statutory and inspection frameworks that you need to be aware of which will affect your planning, delivery and behaviour towards your students. Advancing equality of opportunity means there is the intention to move forward, to get somewhere, to achieve improved outcomes. It's not just about doing things now, but aiming to improve for the future.

Legislation requires organisations to examine their functions, frameworks, services, policies and procedures. They are required to assess whether they could, or do have, a negative impact on people from particular groups who may have been excluded or discriminated against, for example having resources which can be adapted and accessed by all students, perhaps in different formats. It is also important for organisations to examine whether their actions have a positive impact on advancing equality, and to share that good practice internally as well as externally with other agencies and inspection bodies, for example Ofsted. The requirements of inspection bodies should translate into a key strategic aim for your organisation with an action plan which is rigorously monitored. Very clear guidelines should be developed for teachers, setting out what is expected of them and where to go for specialist advice. All staff in your organisation should participate in equality and diversity training. They should understand how to reduce barriers to avoid harassment, victimisation and discrimination against people who have protected characteristics, and how to respond to safe-guarding requirements when teaching young people and vulnerable adults.

As a teacher, it is likely that you will have come across many constraints and barriers that exist for your students. Your expertise in your subject knowledge and practical skills, as well as previous or current diverse work experience, may have been the starting point for your entry to teaching. You will belong to a diverse workforce, particularly where there is an attempt by organisations to represent all protected characteristics. Building your teaching practice on a variety of life and work experiences is a good basis for a common sense approach to equality and diversity. However, responsibility for advancing and applying equality and diversity in an inte-grated way, and taking account of the needs of all students, is being driven at various levels within society. Developing good relations involves tackling prejudice and promoting understanding between students from different groups. Geoff Russell, Chief Executive of the SFA, states:

We are committed to placing equality and diversity at the heart of what we do. There is a direct correlation between skills, productivity and employment. Only by eliminating discrimination and embracing diversity can we ensure that every single person is able to take advantage of the opportunities available to them and make a valuable contribution to the success of this country.

(http://skillsfundingagency.bis.gov.uk/news/pressreleases/
SES+consultation.htm (accessed 03.08.11))

You should embrace the ethos of the statement and place equality and diversity at the heart of your teaching role.

Prejudice and discrimination

Everyone has conscious and unconscious preferences which influence their thoughts (prejudice) and actions (discrimination). It is the unconscious prejudices that can lead people to make prejudgements based on little or no fact, regardless of what is consciously known to be true. The relationship between *prejudice* and *discrimination* will have an impact on your students. There are four main relationships between prejudice and discrimination. The following table gives examples.

You can be prejudiced and discriminatory	You believe that young people in general display offensive behaviour and don't want to learn. You don't teach classes where students are young people.
You can be non-prejudiced yet still discriminate	You believe that there is some good in everyone and that all young people deserve opportunities. Your manager tells you that young people are difficult to work with and best to avoid any teaching which involves this group. You do this because you don't want to contradict him.
You can be prejudiced yet not discriminate	You tell your curriculum manager that you believe he is being discriminatory and he retracts his advice to you. However, he has not changed his mind about young people, he has simply altered his behaviour.
You can be both non-prejudiced and non-discriminatory	You are now both non-prejudiced and non-discriminatory due to your knowledge and experience.

The next activity is the *implicit association* test. You will find the experience interesting and informative and it will give you an insight into the ways in which your unconscious prejudice impacts on your behaviour and ultimately on the way in which you communicate with your students.

Activity

Access the website below and try to describe your self-understanding of one of the topics listed. Then test your conscious versus unconscious preferences ranging from pets to political issues, ethnic groups to sports teams, and entertainers to styles of music. If you are unprepared to encounter interpretations that you might find objectionable, please do not carry out this activity.

https://implicit.harvard.edu/implicit/research/

The results of this activity may tell you something that you are already aware of about yourself or they may give you something to reflect on. The important point is to recognise that judgements are not neutral and that everyone works from a value base. No one exists in a vacuum. This is also an activity you could ask your students to complete, perhaps on their own away from the group environment. If all your students are content to share their findings, it could lead to a useful discussion.

When developing strategies to advance the principles of equality and diversity, you need to have an understanding of where issues such as prejudice and discrimination come from. Prejudices are formed in a number of ways and it is important that you understand these so that they become easier to address should they present themselves when you are teaching. The following diagram by Phil Clements and Tony Spinks explains where some of these come from. They can be planted like a seed and grow deep rooted over time unless tackled.

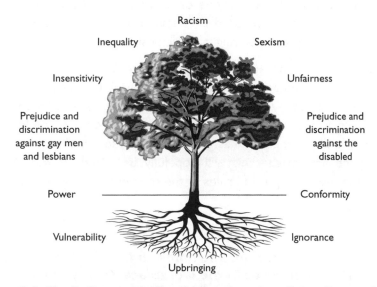

Figure 2.1 Prejudice and discrimination in all its forms has its roots in things we can often, if not always, change, provided we are aware of them. (Clements and Spinks, 2000:10)

Clements and Spinks felt the main roots of prejudice are ignorance, power, vulnerability, upbringing and conformity.

- Ignorance: overcome ignorance by finding out as much as you can about your students before the start of your programme and during the initial assessment process.

- Power: there is power in being the majority in the group. Be aware of the ways in which you are involved in this interaction and reflect what the impact is on your students. You should manage group situations and activities so that all your students have an equal chance to participate and benefit.

- Vulnerability: people cling to what they know for their security so that anything which is different can pose a threat. When a group of students come together who don't know each other and are putting forward their views on aspects of their learning, some may feel threatened by alternative ideas and explanations of how things should or shouldn't be. Encourage your students to share their experiences in a way that avoids making assumptions about their backgrounds. Using an inclusive ice-breaker can help this.

- Upbringing: the influence of your parents, carers and close friends will have had an influence upon your thinking, attitudes, values, beliefs and behaviour. This could be positive or it could be negative. If you had a parent that constantly belittled a certain race, you may subconsciously do the same; however, you might consciously want to do the opposite.

- Conformity: often the need to be liked and to fit in is stronger than the resolve to stand up against attitudes and behaviour which are inappropriate. It is vital that you set an example to your students by challenging this should it arise. By saying or doing nothing you are condoning the behaviour and are therefore as guilty as the person displaying the behaviour in the first place. This will hopefully be raised by your students during the setting of ground rules at the start of the programme.

Example

Lisa teaches Business Administration. She plans and facilitates a discussion based on the students' experiences in the workplace. One student persistently monopolises discussions to the extent that the other students remain quiet and are now reluctant to participate. As well as this, the only views and experiences the group are exposed to are those of the dominant student. This is despite many subtle attempts by Lisa to redress the balance in the group. At this moment the dominant student has the power to drive the discussions during the session.

In this situation Lisa needs to revisit the ground rules established at the start of the programme, and either reinforce or amend them, to enable all students to take part and for learning to be effective. This will help build up the confidence of the other students to participate once more in discussions. In the first instance Lisa could broaden participation by using the students' names. She also needs to tackle the dominant student in a more forthright way, perhaps in a one-to-one discussion. On reflection Lisa needs to consider if she could have prevented this by adopting strategies much earlier on.

Promoting an equal society

The government has actively promoted a more equal society through its policies and through legislative change. The Equality Act 2010 replaced the previous anti-discrimination laws with a single Act. It simplified the law, removed inconsistencies and made it easier for people to understand and comply with it. It also strengthened the law in important ways to help tackle discrimination and inequality. The Equality and Human Rights Commission (EHRC) is the statutory body established to help eliminate discrimination and reduce inequality. It produces practical guidance on how organisations can comply with the Equality Duty and achieve good practice. In April 2011, the public sector Equality Duty came into force in England, Scotland and Wales. This duty replaced the existing race, disability and gender equality duties.

Policies and programmes across the breadth of government aim to improve outcomes for disadvantaged groups and respond to diverse needs, thus reducing the social inequality gap. To help improve the skills of those claiming benefits, conditions could be imposed.

> *Skills Conditionality involves Jobcentre Plus referring those claiming work-related benefits, for example Job Seeker's Allowance, to a skills training provider, further education college or Next Step adviser with potential benefit sanctions for non-participation. The training will include vocational, basic skills, employability training as well as support with softer skills such as motivation and confidence building.*

> (www.dwp.gov.uk/consultations/2010/skills-conditionality.shtml
> (accessed 18.10.11))

You may have students attending your programmes who have been referred by an agency, project or scheme. To help motivate them, try to take account of their interests and needs, and requirements of their workplace if they have a work placement.

Example

Rosie teaches Interview Techniques and Employability Skills to students who are referred through the Work Programme. Each student has their own particular needs in terms of their existing skills and knowledge, and the scope of their work placement. To meet these needs, Rosie negotiates an individual learning programme with each student which also includes a negotiated start and end date.

In this example, Rosie recognises that different students will bring different perspectives, ideas, opinions, histories, faith, skills, knowledge and culture, and that a traditional programme where the start/end date and programme content is the same for all may not meet the needs of individual students in these circumstances. Rosie has shown that she understands how to make adjustments to the programme requirements to suit the student. Students should be invited to discuss any adjustments that may be necessary. They should also be actively involved in making decisions about how they will achieve their learning outcomes and progress towards their planned destination.

Advancing equality and promoting diversity is now everyone's responsibility and organisations must accept that they should seek to promote these through an integrative approach. This will help achieve a more equal society and providing redress for individuals experiencing discrimination is important. Public bodies, such as educational establishments, must proactively eliminate discrimination, harassment and victimisation, rather than waiting for individuals or groups of students (past, present and future) to make a complaint. Organisations should be proactive in advancing equality of opportunity and fostering good relations, not just avoid discrimination or be reactive to situations. For this to be successful, it requires the active support of all personnel, i.e. teaching staff, support staff, volunteers, stakeholders, students, customers and contractors.

You may find that the legislation will have an impact on your students. It may be that the demographics of your group are different from previous groups. You should consider whether you will need to make any adjustments to your programme to ensure your students' experience is effective from their application, through recruitment, initial assessment, induction to teaching and learning approaches, assessment and evaluation.

Activity

Imagine the students you are teaching next time will be predominantly male. You have taught this programme before, mainly to females, and you have all your resources and activities pre-prepared. What adjustments would you make to prepare for your new group and to promote equality and diversity within your teaching?

Learning styles

Most students have a particular learning style, a way that helps them to learn which is based on listening, seeing and doing. Your students could take a short learning styles test prior to commencing your programme to identify what these are. However, what you may tend to do is teach your sessions in the style in which you learn best – although it will suit you, it may not suit your students. Sue Crowley of the IfL stated:

> *Often new teachers teach as they were taught, then perhaps as they would like to have been taught, and finally they realise different people learn in different ways and a wider spectrum of teaching and learning approaches are needed and available.*

(Rose, 2009:8)

Fleming (2005) stated people can be grouped into four styles of learning: visual, aural, read/write and kinaesthetic (VARK).

Visual examples (seeing) – students usually:

- are meticulous and neat in appearance
- find verbal instructions difficult
- memorise by looking at pictures
- notice details
- observe rather than act or talk
- like watching videos/DVDs

Aural examples (listening and talking) – students usually:

- are easily distracted
- enjoy talking and listening to others

- have difficulty with written instructions

- hum, sing and whisper or talk out loud

- ask questions

- don't like noisy environments

Read/write examples (reading and writing) – students usually:

- are good spellers and have good handwriting

- enjoy research

- like rewriting what others have written

- like to read books

- use a dictionary and thesaurus

- write lists and make notes

Kinaesthetic examples (doing) – students usually:

- are tactile towards others

- do not like reading and are often poor spellers

- enjoy worksheets and discussions

- fidget with pens while studying

- like practical activities

- use their hands while talking

Not all students fall into one style; they may be multi-modal, i.e. a mixture of two or more styles enabling learning to take place more quickly. If your students can incorporate *reading, hearing, seeing, saying* and *doing* during your sessions, their learning retention should increase.

Studies show that over a period of three days, learning retention is as follows:

- *10% of what you read*
- *20% of what you hear*
- *30% of what you see*
- *50% of what you see and hear*
- *70% of what you say*
- *90% of what you say and you do*

(Pike, 1989)

Honey and Mumford (1992) suggest students are a mixture of the following four styles:

- activist

- pragmatist

- theorist

- reflector

Activist – students like to deal with new problems and experiences and like lots of activities to keep them busy. They love challenges and are enthusiastic.

Pragmatist – students like to apply what they have learnt to practical situations. They like logical reasons for doing something.

Theorist – students need time to take in information. They prefer to read lots of material first and think about something before applying it. They like things that have been tried and tested.

Reflector – students think deeply about what they are learning and the activities they could do to apply this learning. They will then try something and think again about it.

Activity

Consider something you have recently learnt, for example, using a new mobile phone. Did you: jump right in and press all the buttons (activist); look briefly at the instructions and then have a go (pragmatist); read the instructions thoroughly, then carry them out (theorist); or become confident at using the phone for calls and texts before considering its other uses (reflector)?

It is always useful to get your students to carry out a learning styles test. It can be fun and lead to an interesting discussion, as well as helping you plan your teaching and learning approaches to reach each student's maximum potential.

Activity

If you have access to the internet, log on to the website www.vark-learn. com and carry out the learning styles test. It only takes a few minutes and you will receive an instant result. Locate another suitable learning styles questionnaire and carry it out. Compare and contrast your results. Decide which test could be used with your own students and how you could make use of the results to help their learning. If you don't have internet access, research different learning styles in relevant textbooks.

You may need to consider adjustments to your planning, for example scheme of work, session plans and teaching methods depending on the preferred learning styles of your students. It may be that you will find male students prefer to learn by doing (kinaesthetic) and that your existing programme planning does not reflect this. If the gender make-up of the group is different from the previous time you delivered this programme, then you will need to explore what adjustments can be made. This may also involve reviewing the use of any specialist staff, guest speakers or other agencies involved. You might need to amend your handouts, presentations and activities to reflect both genders.

Extension Activity

All agendas for team meetings should include an item for equality and diversity. At the next meeting, ask if you can present a resource which you have amended to suit the needs of different students. Be prepared to explain your rationale (who, what, when, where, why and how) and what impact it will have/has had on the progress of your students. Further develop this into a case study which your organisation could present as evidence as part of an Ofsted inspection or audit.

Advancing equality

The fundamental reason for advancing equality is to meet the needs of individual students so that they will achieve improved outcomes. Individuals are at the heart of the education system, and meeting their needs requires an active approach to equality of opportunity at all stages of their learning journey. It is about the removal of social and economic barriers to participation. Good equal opportunities practices ensure that all students:

- are respected and not discriminated against

- become aware of equality and inclusion

- benefit from high quality opportunities to learn and achieve

- learn in an environment that supports their development

The SFA and YPLA look to employers and learning organisations they fund to advance equality of opportunity, widen participation and improve outcomes for students. They commit to the following explicit and implicit references.

Explicit references:

- a zero tolerance approach should be taken to any discrimination, victimisation, bullying or harassment

- equality of opportunity should be advanced, and discrimination tackled so that all students achieve their potential

- guidance and support should be sensitive to equality of opportunity

- organisations should have effective measures to eliminate oppressive behaviour, including all forms of harassment, bullying and victimisation

- programmes should be socially inclusive, ensuring equality of access and opportunities for students

- teachers should use materials and teaching methods that advance equality of opportunity

- there should be explicit aims, values and strategies advancing equality for all that are reflected in the organisation's work

Implicit references:

- students should have access to relevant, effective support on personal issues

- students should understand their rights and responsibilities

- learning resources and accommodation should allow all students to participate fully

- organisations should promote good working relationships that foster learning

- programmes should be responsive to local need

- the organisation's values should be fully understood by staff, including subcontractors, employers and work placement organisations

- the performance of different groups of students should be used to guide programme development

You need to take positive steps to advance equality and diversity in everything you do that may affect the learning experience. Try to be proactive and meet your students' needs as soon as you become aware of them.

Example

Kevin has declared to you during his initial interview that he is transgender and is about to undertake gender reassignment treatment. He wants to know which toilet facilities he can use. He has not asked that this information remain confidential.

This declaration by your student means that your whole organisation is *deemed to know* under the Equality Act 2010 and will need to make *reasonable adjustments* so that Kevin has access to toilet facilities he is comfortable with. It might be suggested by your organisation that Kevin can use the disabled toilet which is accessed by both males and females. If your organisation is unable to respond to Kevin's needs, he may feel that under the Equality Act 2010, his needs have not been given the same consideration as those of male and female gender. Taking positive action may be a way of avoiding unlawful discrimination, i.e. providing support for a student who is undergoing gender reassignment.

The following table gives some practical suggestions you could use to advance equality.

Marketing and recruitment	Actively market to under-represented groups as identified by government policies and through local knowledge of your communities. Ensure all promotional materials are inclusive and do not stereotype. Ensure application forms gather equal opportunities data, also known as *impact data*. This data must be used for the sole purpose of monitoring and kept completely separate from any decisions regarding the recruitment process. Ensure your equal opportunities policy is explicit in any marketing and recruitment materials and practice, and in early discussions with your students.

Induction and initial assessment	Carry out relevant initial assessment and diagnostic tests. Check that your students and any support staff understand the equality and diversity policies and procedures, act on them and know where they can be accessed. Consider how effective teaching and learning is for your students, following analysis of their initial assessment tests and identification of their learning styles. Consider how well your students are guided and supported. Ensure the learning environment is welcoming to all, irrespective of age, disability, gender reassignment, pregnancy or maternity, race, religion or belief, sex and sexual orientation. Find out from your students if they require any adjustments to be made to the environment, equipment or resources. If so, ensure this is carried out. Identify and remove barriers within your control, which hinder or prevent students from achieving their full potential. Inform students of who they can contact in case of a query or problem, for example your organisation's Designated Safeguarding Officer. Respect confidentiality at all times.
Teaching and learning	Consider how well your programme and activities meet the needs and interests of all your students. Ensure all teaching and learning materials are inclusive and adaptable, use clear language and don't contain too much jargon. Ensure the environment is free from potential hazards, for example by moving bags and coats out of the way. Make arrangements to meet cultural, religious or faith needs. Prepare well in advance to make adjustments to programme requirements and session plans. Provide adapted materials where needed. Seek opportunities within your programme delivery to celebrate cultural diversity, widen your students' cultural understanding and prepare them to be effective citizens in a diverse society. Participate in local events linking them to learning programmes or a diversity calendar. Take positive action to provide individual encouragement and support to all students. Talk to students for whom adjustments have been made, to ensure these are successful. Utilise support services within the organisation.

Assessment	Ensure that your assessment methods follow the rules of VACSR (valid, authentic, current, sufficient and reliable).
	Find out what the awarding organisation's policy is with regard to access to assessment.
	Know what adjustments to make to assessments and examinations to enable all your students to have the opportunity to achieve their potential.
	Liaise with others as necessary.
Evaluation	Consult with students who have received additional support to obtain feedback regarding their experience, and use the outcomes to guide further action.
	Evaluate the impact of your sessions on the effective implementation of equality and diversity policies, and whether they are embracing inclusivity.
	Obtain feedback from your students to show that adjustments have been implemented.

Activity

Look at the previous table and identify any aspects which you (or your organisation) do not currently do. Could you do anything differently?

Make a list of good practice points which can be used to ensure students receive the information they need throughout their learning journey.

Some students may not want to complete the section on their application form which asks them to disclose details such as a disability, ethnic origin, date of birth, etc. They are not required to do so; however, the information will help your organisation support students with any reasonable adjustments which might be required, as well as collect data for purposes such as funding, and statistics to inform policies. Demonstrating an inclusive learning environment will encourage students to consider your organisation as they will want to learn in an environment which is already inclusive.

Tackling inequality is about social justice and the rationale for dealing with it is based on developing a fairer society. This argument is based on the belief that everyone should have a right to equal access to employment. When employed, they should have equal pay and equal access to training and development, as well as being free of any direct or indirect discrimination and victimisation, harassment or bullying. This can be described as *the right to be treated fairly*, and your organisation should aim to:

- advance equality of *opportunity*, i.e. ensure that students have the freedom to follow their own learning style, and have the chance to take an appropriate programme

- advance equality of *outcome*, i.e. ensure that students have an equal chance of achievement

- advance equality of *process*, i.e. treat students according to their individual needs through teaching and learning

- widen participation opportunities to reach all areas of the local community and society

It is important that your organisation has a consistent approach to dealing with victimisation, harassment and discrimination. This will make it easier for teachers and students to identify and change unfair practices. It is your responsibility to manage the learning experience and deal with any inequalities that occur.

Dr Morris Massey (2008), an American psychologist, carried out research regarding how values are formed and what they mean. He stated that by the time we reach 21 our value system is more or less fixed. However, it can be changed if you experience a *Significant Emotional Event*, for example birth, death, divorce, etc. It does not have to be a dramatic event, but something that is really memorable, for example an exciting learning experience. You may have heard your students describe their learning as *something that has changed their lives*. This demonstrates the impact that a positive learning experience has had on your students. Conversely a bad learning experience can have an effect through some form of inequality or discrimination.

Attitudes affecting behaviour

Good teachers are often described by students as having a huge impact on their attitude and behaviour as a result of a good learning experience. These teachers are positive role models, having reached their students on an individual basis. The most affected students might not have engaged with education in their past, perhaps had a bad learning experience or a poor teacher.

Betari's Cycle, also known as Betari's Box, is about how attitude affects behaviour. For example, my attitude affects my behaviour, which affects your attitude which affects your behaviour, which in turn affects my attitude and so on. It's not clear where the name Betari came from; however, attitudes, whether positive or negative, are reflected in behaviour. Positive attitudes should encourage positive behaviour in yourself, as well as in others. This can be through words and actions, verbal and non-verbal messages, and body language.

Figure 2.2 Betari's Cycle

Example

Gemma enjoys her ICT classes. She is a kinaesthetic learner and often learns new word-processing functions by making mistakes and then correcting her actions. Today, she has a different teacher, Abi, as her usual teacher is absent. Abi is quick to notice when Gemma is struggling and takes over her mouse to choose the correct functions. This continues throughout the session, therefore Gemma now stops when she is unsure of something and calls over Abi. Because of Abi's attitude and behaviour towards Gemma's learning, Gemma has adapted her attitude and behaviour to fit in with Abi.

To change the attitude and behaviour of others you need to be aware of your own attitude and how it affects your own behaviour. You can then notice how your behaviour affects other people's attitudes and behaviour. You can break the cycle by noticing how the behaviour of others makes you feel and refusing to let it affect you. You need to recognise negative cycles and turn them into positive ones. This applies to yourself as well as your students.

Before the start of your programme, you should be proactive in thinking about what you need to do to advance equality in your teaching practice. Having a positive attitude towards teaching your students will help influence their attitudes and behaviour. Try to develop your ability to embrace opportunities as they arise and to challenge your students as a key learning opportunity for all. Make sure you consider your behaviour towards equality and diversity throughout your planning, delivery, assessment and when creating and using resources.

- Planning: is there anything in the environment that makes it inaccessible for any students? Have you included opportunities for differentiated activities in your scheme of work?

- Delivery: can you incorporate naturally occurring opportunities for discussion within your session planning such as Chinese New Year or Hindu New Year?

- Assessment: can you use a different assessment method, i.e. asking oral questions rather than using written questions for a student who struggles with reading and writing?

- Resources: are people from diverse backgrounds, including socio-economic and cultural, and people with disabilities visible in your programme materials?

Addressing inequality throughout your teaching and the use of resources will help you deal with any issues as they arise to make improvements for the future. You could create an equality and diversity improvement plan which will list the resources you intend to change with target dates and actions required. By carrying out an evaluation of your actions you should be able to analyse whether these improvements have had a positive impact on your programme's retention and achievement rates. You can also gain feedback and data from student questionnaires. This information will be collated by your organisation and used by funding bodies such as the SFA and Ofsted to measure the overall effectiveness of your students' journey.

The following are some simple behaviour strategies you could use with your students to advance equality:

- use a suitable and inclusive icebreaker

- negotiate and agree appropriate ground rules

- learn students' names and use them regularly along with eye contact

- allocate time during the induction process for information and discussions regarding equality and diversity

- make sure everyone is aware of your organisation's policies

- schedule one-to-one discussions with students who require additional support at the beginning and throughout the programme

- hold group and individual tutorials with all students to discuss progress and concerns

- gain feedback from your students about their experiences at strategic points throughout the programme, i.e. after induction, mid way and at the end

- create an equality and diversity improvement plan to reflect changes you could make based on situations which have arisen

Activity

Carry out an evaluation of the materials you have used for a particular programme with a focus on equality and diversity. Check your scheme of work, session plans and resources to see what you could change. Create an equality and diversity improvement plan to implement the next time you teach this programme.

Types of behaviour

There may be occasions during your sessions where behaviours exist that are offensive, directly discriminate or are distressing to others. This behaviour may be obvious, but it can also be unintentional and subtle. It might involve nicknames, teasing, name-calling or excluding someone, which is not with malicious intent but which is nevertheless upsetting. If this should happen in your group of students it is your organisation's responsibility, through you, to tackle any inappropriate comments or behaviour. All organisations need to examine existing arrangements to ensure they advance fairness and equality. Dr Christine Rose defines direct discrimination as that which occurs when:

> Someone is treated unfairly, or less favourably than another person, because they have a protected characteristic. This often arises because of assumptions, stereotyping or prejudice. Direct discrimination also covers association discrimination or perception discrimination. This is direct discrimination against someone because they associate with a person who has the protected characteristic or because they are perceived to have a protected characteristic.

(2010: 4)

You need to know what steps your organisation requires you to take to prevent discrimination, and take this action when inappropriate behaviour occurs. There are various ways of managing this depending on the circumstances:

- establish what is acceptable behaviour at the start of the programme

- embrace student diversity within the group

- create an acceptable behaviour contract which students sign up to and revisit it regularly – perhaps as part of the ground rules

- challenge prejudice, discrimination and stereotyping as it happens

- encourage your students to confidentially discuss any behaviour during the programme that may give them cause for concern

- ensure all resources are inclusive through the use of positive images or the imaginative production of those resources (Braille, diagrams, cartoons, etc.)

- if any students intend to leave, or have left, find out why

- plan the integration of equality and diversity in your programme delivery

Example

Jerome has attended a week's summer school programme as part of his PGCE. All students were required to give the teacher their name, telephone number and relationship of an emergency contact. The completed forms were left on the teacher's desk where they could be seen by other students. As a result it becomes common knowledge among the group that Jerome has a same sex partner. Jerome became distressed and left the programme.

You are required to treat personal information in the strictest confidence and your students will trust you with details about their private lives. Information about students should not become common knowledge via their teacher. The impact on this student is that he was unable to achieve his qualification. This situation constitutes harassment and/or a breach of the Data Protection Act (1998).

Extension Activity

Has your organisation been involved in a process of self-assessment to report their activities and performance? If so, find out how you can access the report and action plan. Look at how the information is represented in the report. Do you recognise the data being presented? Have you been asked to contribute to this process? Do the strengths and weaknesses reflect your evaluation of your programme and students? What about the improvement plan – does it contain similar areas to the ones you've identified as needing to improve?

Benefits of diversity

Diversity may be considered in terms of demographics (gender, age, ethnicity) but also in terms of skills, background, experience, attitude, personality, work, experience and understanding. It is about visible and non-visible differences. While equality is about treating everyone equally in terms of rights, status and opportunities, with an emphasis on eradicating discrimination, diversity is about making sure that everyone is valued and included.

The Chartered Institute of Personnel and Development states:

> *Everyone is a unique person. Even though people have things in common with each other they are also different in all sorts of ways. Differences include visible and non-visible factors, for example, personal characteristics such as background, culture, personality, and work-style, size, accent, language and so on. A number of personal characteristics are covered by discrimination law to give people protection against being treated unfairly. The 'protected characteristics' are race, disability, gender reassignment, sex, marriage and civil partnership, pregnancy and maternity, religion and belief, sexual orientation and age.*

> *CIPD defines managing diversity as valuing everyone as an individual – valuing people as employees, customers and clients.*

> *It is important to recognise that a 'one-size-fits all' approach to managing people does not achieve fairness and equality of opportunity for everyone. People have different personal needs, values and beliefs. Good people management practice demands that people propositions are both consistently fair but also flexible and inclusive in ways that are designed to support business needs.*

> (www.cipd.co.uk/subjects/dvsequl/general/divover.htm
> (accessed 03.08.11))

Having a diverse group of staff puts an organisation in a stronger position to meet the needs of their diverse students, offer a richer and more effective learning experience and provide positive role models. However, many organisations continue to take a compliance only approach to the issue of diversity from the top down, thus missing out on benefits, such as improved creativity, innovation and customer service that arise from a more wholehearted approach to diversity. Successful organisations will recognise the need for immediate action and are ready and willing to spend resources on managing diversity.

In this respect, your students will benefit from:

- a greater understanding of the diverse groups of potential and existing students represented, meeting their needs more effectively

- a greater variety of solutions to problems

- better communication with diverse groups of potential and existing students

- greater access to a wider range of individual strengths, experiences, talents and ideas through a diverse collection of skills and perspectives

- varying points of view providing a larger pool of ideas and experiences

Diversity in the Lifelong Learning Sector includes all types of students engaging in a wide number of subject specialist areas and disciplines. The benefit of this will lead to a greater number of people from different backgrounds being able to seek an education.

Andragogy and pedagogy

Andragogy, initially defined as *the art and science of helping adults learn* by Malcolm Knowles (1913–1997), currently defines an alternative to *pedagogy* (traditional teacher-centred learning) and refers to student-focused education for people of all ages. In other words, an andragogical approach is all about giving the student control of their own learning. In the past, students who could not fit into the pedagogical formal learning system were shunned as they were considered difficult. As a result many people did not succeed within the education framework because they were not taught according to their learning styles or perceptive skills. For example, people with autism have been found to focus on the tiny details of information rather than the bigger picture, as the average person might.

Students are now more involved with negotiating and directing their learning. Teachers should adapt their teaching methods to take account of the needs of all their students ensuring the learning environment fits with the students and not the other way round. The benefit here is that more students engage in educational activities and stay with their learning until they have achieved their aim.

A diverse group of students can be a valuable educational resource that enhances the learning experience. You should try to gain a sense of how your students feel about the cultural climate in your group and encourage your students to explore perspectives outside of their own experiences. Providing opportunities for all your students to get to know each other will enable them to recognise diverse backgrounds and special interests. During group discussions, scenarios, case studies and feedback from activities your students will have the opportunity to listen and become more informed about cultures and faiths other than their own. Embracing diversity encourages your students to overcome their stereotypes and biases.

Activity

Review the systems and structures within your organisation which promote equality and value diversity. Identify those which you think are working and those which are not. What do you think the challenges are for your organisation and what impact will this have on individuals?

Taking full advantage of the benefits of diversity is not without its challenges. Some of these are as follows.

- *Communication*: perceptual, cultural, dialect and language barriers need to be overcome for diversity to succeed. Try to foster an attitude of openness by encouraging all students to express their ideas and opinions and attribute an equal sense of value to all.

- *Resistance to change*: there are always some students and staff who will refuse to accept the fact that the social and cultural make-up of society is changing. The notion of the *we've always done it this way attitude* inhibits new ideas and progress. This can be counteracted by involving all students and staff in creating and implementing diversity initiatives in your learning environment.

There can still be diversity even when there is not a significant minority group, as all individuals are different. Diversity not only involves how people perceive themselves but how they perceive others and those perceptions affect their interactions and beliefs.

Extension Activity

Reflect on how aware you are of the aspirations and goals of your current students. Ask yourself the following questions about your students and their learning programme:

- *What are their aspirations and will this programme help achieve them?*

- *Is the programme planning and delivery realistic and relevant?*

- *How will I know if they are achieving and moving further along their journey?*

- *How effectively are they prepared for their next step after the programme?*

- *Does the programme content reflect what they will find in their chosen career?*

- *Have I looked at this programme through the eyes of each and every student?*

If you can't successfully answer all the questions, set yourself an action plan to ensure you can.

Summary

In this chapter you have learnt about:

- applying the principles of equality and diversity

- advancing equality

- benefits of diversity

Cross-referencing grid

This chapter contributes towards the following: scope (S), knowledge (K) and practice (P) aspects of the Professional Teaching Standards (A–F domains) and the Equality and Diversity assessment criteria at levels 3 and 4. Full details of the learning outcomes and assessment criteria for the units can be found in the appendices.

Domain	Standards
A	AS3, AK3.1, AP3.1
B	BS1, BS5, BK1.2, BK5.2, BP1.2, BP5.2
C	
D	DS1, DK1.1, DP1.1
E	ES2, EK2.1, EP2.1
F	
Equality and Diversity unit	**Assessment criteria**
Level 3	2.1, 2.2, 2.3, 3.1, 4.1, 4.2, 5.1
Level 4	2.1, 2.2, 2.3, 3.1, 4.1, 4.2, 5.1

Theory focus

References and further information

Clements, P and Spinks, T (2000) *The Equal Opportunities Handbook: How to Recognise Diversity, Encourage Fairness and Promote Anti-Discriminatory Practice: How to Deal with Everyday Issues of Unfairness* (3rd edn). London: Kogan Page

Fleming, N (2005) *Teaching and learning styles: VARK strategies*. Honolulu: Honolulu Community College

Honey, P and Mumford, A (1992) *The manual of learning styles* (3rd edn). Maidenhead: Peter Honey Associates

IODA (2010) *Diversity Fairness and Equality Information Booklet*. Tadcaster: IODA Limited

Learning and Skills Council (2007) *Single Equality Scheme: Our Strategy for Equality and Diversity*. Coventry: Learning and Skills Council

Massey, M, in IODA (2008) *Diversity, Fairness and Equality Information Booklet*. Tadcaster: IODA Limited

Pike, R W (1989) *Creative Training Techniques Handbook*. Minneapolis MN: Lakewood Books

Rose, C (2010) *Brief Guide: Equality Act 2010*. Coventry: Learning and Skills Improvement Service (LSIS)

Rose, C (2009) *Equality, Diversity and Governance in Further Education Colleges*. Coventry: Learning and Skills Improvement Service (LSIS)

Websites

Chartered Institute for Professional Development – Diversity in the workplace – www.cipd.co.uk/subjects/dvsequl/general/divover.htm

Data Protection Act (2003) – http://regulatorylaw.co.uk/Data_Protection_Act_2003.html

Equality and Human Rights Commission (EHRC) – www.equalityhumanrights.com

Equality Duty – www.equalityhumanrights.com/advice-and-guidance/public-sector-equality-duty/

Knowles, M: Andragogy and Pedagogy – www.infed.org/thinkers/et-knowl.htm

Learning styles test – www.vark-learn.com

Ofsted – www.ofsted.gov.uk

Skills Funding Agency – www.skillsfundingagency.bis.gov.uk

Young People's Learning Agency – www.ypla.gov.uk

Introduction

In this chapter you will learn about:

- demonstrating good practice
- adapting learning situations and resources
- developing strategies for dealing with discrimination

There are activities and examples which will help you reflect on the above and assist your understanding of how to demonstrate appropriate behaviour. At the end of each section is an extension activity to stretch and challenge your learning further.

At the end of the chapter, there is a cross-referencing grid showing how the content of this chapter contributes towards the Professional Teaching Standards and the Equality and Diversity assessment criteria at levels 3 and 4. There is also a theory focus with relevant references, further information and websites you might like to refer to.

Demonstrating good practice

It is important to recognise that to demonstrate good practice in equality and diversity with maximum impact for your students, it needs to be embedded throughout the culture of your organisation. Equality and diversity policies need to be well known and practised by all staff. This should enable your organisation to respond to issues of diversity, differences and inequalities among students, staff and the local community. Policies should be regularly reviewed and underpin a flexible programme that identifies individual and local/community requirements and can be adapted to meet changing needs.

Teaching will bring you face to face with many diverse situations, environments and people. Depending upon where you teach, you may experience students:

- aged 14 upwards

- whose first language is not English

- who are currently in prison, on remand or recently released

- who are immigrants

- who are transient

- who have had negative experiences of education in the past

- who have mobility, physical, mental or learning difficulties

- who have undergone gender reassignment

A good first impression will help establish a positive working relationship with your students. The way you dress, act, respond to questions, offer support, etc. will also influence your students. They don't need to know anything personal about you, but they will probably make assumptions about you. If asked personal questions, try not to give out any information. By remaining a professional, and not becoming too friendly, you will retain their respect. Establishing routines will help your sessions flow smoothly, for example always starting on time, setting and keeping to time limits for activities and breaks, and finishing on time.

Activity

Think about the subject you will teach, the age group of your students and the environment in which you will teach. What do you consider are ways of demonstrating good practice and why?

Information for students

Your students' experiences of your organisation may have already begun before they arrive for their first session. They may have obtained information perhaps from a brochure or website, or may have visited the organisation and already met some of the staff. Equality and diversity practices need to be embedded across the organisation to enable students to start their journey with an open and inclusive learning experience from their first welcome to their completion.

Example

An information leaflet for prospective students includes details of crèche provision. Many students come to the centre whose first language is not English, and who do not have other childcare arrangements. This leaflet is therefore not accessible to these students. Following an analysis of languages spoken in this community, the leaflet has now been produced in two other languages.

Meeting the potential needs of students, even before they commence, will help remove any possible barriers. Other barriers could include transport, access or finance. If funding was available, organisations could help with these and advertise details of how they can help. Students should not be accepted onto a programme purely because a certain number are needed for it to run. This is not fair to them and they may leave as a result. You might need to allow more time for the enrolment process if required. This will ensure your students are on the right programme and able to achieve. You might need to use translation services and liaise with others to organise a support worker with expertise in a particular learning disability if necessary.

Activity

Analyse how accessible the programme information for prospective students is at your organisation. Is information produced or available in different formats to meet potential varying needs of students? How proactive is your organisation in promoting this and what could be changed to improve it?

Student details

Before the commencement of your programme, you need to find out if any of your students have already shared information and details about themselves to someone in your organisation. They may have previously attended a programme in another subject area. If they have completed an enrolment form they should have been asked if they wish to disclose any learning difficulty or disability. At this first stage some students will willingly share this information and some will not. Some students may not see themselves as having a *disability* but recognise that they have particular requirements or needs. If a student has been disadvantaged in the past, they may not tell anyone in these early stages about difficulties they may have. However, if a student does disclose a disability or additional requirements to one person, the whole organisation is *deemed to know*. Before the student embarks on their learning, you need to create an atmosphere whereby your students feel they can talk to you in confidence. If they want to tell you about any particular requirements or if they have any needs they feel are not being addressed it's important they can talk to you. Your student might tell you that they don't want anyone else to know about their learning difficulty or disability. However, this makes it difficult for you to put in place appropriate reasonable adjustments for that student, and you would tactfully need to discuss this with them to reach an appropriate outcome.

Students will feel much more confident about disclosure from the beginning if they feel that you and the organisation as a whole have a positive and supportive attitude towards anyone who has any additional requirements. All organisations must take *reasonable steps* to encourage disclosure. It is good practice to:

- talk to your students to find out how you can help them;

- find out how long any necessary adjustments will take to implement and follow up where necessary;

- keep your student informed about progress and timescales.

Example

Sara told her teacher during her interview that she has Asperger's Syndrome, and finds it difficult to sit still for long periods of time. She doesn't want the others in the group to know about this. Her teacher asked her how he could help her and discussed various options. He reassured her that there will be plenty of practical activities involving moving around the learning environment during the sessions.

It may be that further into the programme once the student gets to know the others she will feel comfortable disclosing this information, but for now a *reasonable adjustment* was negotiated that she is comfortable with. The impact in this particular example is that the student will come to the first session less worried than she would have otherwise been, and enjoy an effective and relaxed learning experience. It is important that this process is documented in the student's records or individual learning plan, as well as your own planning documentation. It will provide evidence of the steps you've taken should it be required and, more importantly, demonstrate any impact on the student.

Student support and learning support

Students will not always disclose, or perhaps even recognise, that they have any particular requirements. Getting to know your students will help you identify any requirements they may have so you are able to support them appropriately. *Student support* is generic support relating to the learning experience, for example advice, counselling, crèche, study skills, etc. *Learning support* is specific support relating to the achievement of the qualification such as literacy, numeracy and Information and Communication Technology (ICT). Inclusion involves ensuring that all support systems are available to those students who need such support.

Example

Chris knows he has difficulty with spelling, is embarrassed by this, and therefore hasn't informed his teacher. In group work he always offers to do the oral feedback and has become very adept at side-stepping any written tasks.

If producing written evidence is an important activity and is assessed as part of your programme, then you would need to plan this in the various activities you will use.

Your organisation should have support mechanisms to meet any special requirements or individual needs of students.

Examples of support include the following.

- Dyspraxia – allow additional time and space if necessary for students who have poor motor co-ordination.

- Dysgraphia – allow the use of a computer or other suitable media for students who have difficulty with handwriting.

- Dyscalculia – allow additional time if necessary and use calculators or other equipment for students who have difficulty with calculations or mathematics.

- Dyslexia – allow additional time or resources if necessary for students who have difficulty processing language. Present written questions in a more simplified format, for example bullet points. Ask questions verbally and make an audio or visual recording of your student's responses; allow the use of a laptop for typing responses rather than expecting handwritten responses.

- A disability – students could be taught in a more comfortable environment where appropriate access and support systems are available. Students could be given extra time to complete assessment tasks, or to take medication privately. Dates could be rearranged to fit around doctor or hospital appointments.

- A hearing impairment – an induction loop could be used. Instructions and questions could be conveyed using sign language.

- A visual impairment – use large print or Braille; use specialist computer software if available; ask questions verbally.

- Varying work patterns – try to schedule learning and assessment at a time and place to suit.

- English as a second or other language – use interpreters. Many awarding organisations can translate assessment materials if requested. Bilingual assessments should also be offered.

Example

If you have a student with dyslexia ask them if they would prefer handouts on coloured paper. For a student who is visually impaired you could use resources in a larger font or they could use a magnified reading lamp. For a hearing impaired student, you could give a written test instead of an oral test. For a student with Asperger's syndrome, you could use written questions rather than oral questions. For some students who might struggle with spelling and grammar, the use of a computer could help. An adapted keyboard or a pen grip could help a student with arthritis.

Always ask your students how you can support them, but try to avoid making them feel different, embarrassed or uncomfortable. For example, you could give all students in the group a handout on coloured paper so as not to draw attention to the one student with dyslexia in the group. The Equality Act (2010) requires organisations to make reasonable adjustments where necessary. Don't just assume you have to carry out any amendment to provision on your own; there should be specialist staff to help.

Examples of learning support include:

- literacy;
- numeracy;
- ICT;
- study skills.

Initial assessment

This is the formal way of ascertaining your students' prior skills and/or knowledge of the subject to be taken and whether they have any specific needs that should be taken into account to help them meet the qualification requirements. It should be carried out prior to or at the beginning of the programme. There could be particular entry requirements for your subject and an initial assessment or interview would ascertain if these had been met. *Diagnostic* assessments can be used to evaluate a student's skills, knowledge, strengths and areas for development in a particular area. It could be that your student feels they are capable of achieving at a higher level than the initial assessments determine. The results will give a thorough indication of not only the level at which your student needs to be placed for their subject but also which specific aspects they need to improve on. Diagnostic tests can also be used to ascertain information regarding literacy, numeracy and computer skills. Information gained from these tests will help you plan your sessions to meet any individual needs and/or to arrange further training and support if necessary.

Using initial assessments will help you to identify any particular aspects which may otherwise go unnoticed and ensure you are meeting equality and diversity requirements.

Initial assessment will:

- allow for differentiation and individual requirements to be met
- ensure students are on the right programme at the right level
- ensure students know what is expected of them
- identify an appropriate starting point for each student
- identify an appropriate pace at which each student will progress
- identify any information which needs to be shared with colleagues
- identify any specific additional support needs or special requirements
- identify learning styles
- identify previous experience, achievements and transferable skills
- identify specific requirements, for example literacy, numeracy and ICT skills
- inspire and motivate students
- involve students, giving them confidence to agree suitable targets

The results of initial assessments should help you agree individual learning plans (ILPs) or action plans with your students, ensuring they are on the right programme at the right level.

Activity

Find out what the initial and diagnostic assessment process involves at your organisation. How can you effectively use the information you receive? What student support and learning support is available? How can your students access it? Is information available via notice boards, the intranet, in leaflets, etc. which could be displayed in different languages and formats? Make sure your students are aware of what is available to them.

Inclusive learning

Inclusive learning is about recognising that each of your students is different and that this is the starting point for developing and planning their learning programme. You should plan your teaching and learning sessions to enable all of your students to take part, and at the end of the programme achieve their learning goals. This involves identifying their generic and specific needs, providing appropriate resources and support, meeting their preferred learning styles and encouraging them to try new ones, and giving access to fair assessment.

Your students should always be placed at the heart of everything you do and the policies, procedures and systems put in place by your organisation should support this. This is known as a *student-centred* approach. The Tomlinson Report (1996) promoted a *student-centred* approach that makes students' individual needs the starting point of the teaching and learning process. Instead of your student having to fit in with existing provision being offered by learning providers, Tomlinson makes the case for fitting the provision around the needs of your student:

> By inclusive learning we mean the greatest degree of match or fit between how students learn best, what they need and want to learn, and what is required from the sector, a college and teachers for successful learning to take place.

(Tomlinson Report 1996: 2)

The inclusive approach should help you demonstrate good practice and advance equality of opportunity for all students towards improved outcomes. A quick response to addressing any specific needs is vital to building the confidence of your students and maintaining their motivation. You should create an understanding of and communication between all your students, to embrace and advance equality and diversity within your organisation.

The aim is not for students to simply take part in further education but to be actively included and fully engaged in their learning. At the heart of our thinking lies the idea of match or fit between how the student learns best, what they need and want to learn and what is required from the FE sector, the college and teachers for successful learning to take place.

(Tomlinson, 1996: 2)

When planning your sessions you should:

- identify and organise specialist help and be aware of any student support needed outside of the teaching environment, for example access to refreshment areas, toilets, parking, etc.

- ensure the day/time does not clash with other events which the student may already be committed to, for example a weekly event held for those with learning difficulties or for literacy support; be aware of the bigger community picture in your planning

- plan to use a variety of teaching methods taking account of learning preferences and student destinations

- create, design and/or select/adapt appropriate resources and activities

- encourage social, cultural and recreational activities relevant to the programme (if applicable)

- ensure that all students are included in group activities and be aware of how group dynamics can sometimes exclude an individual

- organise individual arrangements in good time for examinations or assessments, for example, apply to awarding organisations for approval where extra time is needed

- provide opportunities for feedback, comments and suggestions

You should be *proactive* when planning, and provide an inclusive and flexible learning environment, rather than being *reactive* to situations. This will help advance equality of opportunity in all aspects of the learning experience.

Activity

Consider how you would promote inclusive learning and how you could advance equality of opportunity throughout your teaching to improve outcomes for your students. How would you give support for and due regard to:

- *any specific learning difficulties and/or disabilities*

- *any generic student needs*

- *students who do not disclose they have a particular requirement*

- *any occurrences of discrimination or stereotyping*

- *any language barriers*

When teaching, you should always ensure you:

- are non-judgemental

- challenge any direct or indirect discrimination, stereotyping, prejudice, harassment, bullying and biased attitudes by yourself or others

- challenge your own values, attitudes and beliefs so that you are not imposing these upon your students

- do not have favourite students or give some more attention than others

- do not indulge the minority at the expense of the majority

- ensure particular groups are not offended, for example faiths or religions

- ensure particular students are not disadvantaged or overly advantaged

- treat all students with respect and dignity

- use activities and assessments which are pitched at the right level and cover all learning styles

- use questions which are worded so as not to cause embarrassment to students

You should try to embed the Equality Act's nine protected characteristics within your resources and your practice. They are:

- age

- disability

- gender

- gender identity

- marriage and civil partnership

- maternity and pregnancy

- race

- religion and belief

- sexual orientation

For example:

- use pictures to represent each characteristic in your resources and on publicity and marketing materials

- discuss issues based around them when they arise during your sessions, such as their perceptions of disability, older people, different races, etc.

- draw upon the experiences of students within your group and mix different students during group and paired activities

- embrace differences and celebrate events

- encourage research activities which relate your subject to the characteristics

- create crosswords, word searches, puzzles or quizzes based around the characteristics

Besides planning to embed aspects within your sessions, you should use naturally occurring opportunities whenever they arise during your sessions.

Example

Leah was teaching a group of Hair and Beauty students who were three weeks into a two-year day release programme. There were 12 females and two males. During a group activity, Leah overheard one of the females make a remark that the males must be gay if they were taking this programme. After the activity, Leah took the opportunity to open up a group discussion as to why the perception was that males must be gay if they are in the hair and beauty profession. Leah ensured each student was able to voice their opinion and by the end of the session the perception had changed.

Staff development

Organisations should invest in equality and diversity development and training for all staff; this will create a culture of support and commitment by all. It is crucial that you participate in the building of strong teams within your organisation to support one another. Attending staff training and keeping up to date with equality and diversity issues will raise your awareness and confidence to respond to your students' particular needs, along with any discriminatory or challenging behaviour.

Staff development, training and information might be incorporated into:

- a virtual learning environment (VLE) if used
- curriculum and team meetings
- external quality assurance
- internal quality assurance and standardisation meetings
- mentoring
- peer support and/or observations
- programme and curriculum reviews
- staff briefings, one-day training sessions, conferences and seminars
- staff induction
- the intranet, information leaflets and staff handbook

As a teacher you are required to maintain your CPD to keep up to date with your subject area, and generic skills and knowledge such as amendments/additions to legislation and changes to awarding organisation procedures. This should be documented and reflected upon (see Chapter 5 for more information regarding CPD). If you are required to register with the IfL, the professional body for teachers, they require you to complete 30 hours of CPD per year, pro-rata based on the number of hours you teach.

Example

At Ibrahim's recent appraisal, he felt he needed training regarding diversity in the learning environment to help him improve outcomes for his students. He will therefore attend a session to update his knowledge, put into practice what he has learnt and reflect upon the impact of this.

CPD will help you improve your own attitudes and behaviour, to ultimately improve your students' experience, their attitude and their behaviour. You will also have the opportunity to reflect on how this will impact on your professional role as a teacher. Participation in CPD activities provides a good forum for you to use your reflective thinking. There is a checklist for advancing equality and diversity in Appendix 5 which will help develop your practice.

Extension Activity

You might consider that you are demonstrating appropriate behaviour throughout the teaching and learning cycle. However, your colleagues might use different approaches and behaviours which you could learn from. Ask if you can carry out some observations of your peers and discuss their approaches to each aspect of the teaching and learning cycle. Critically evaluate what you could now do differently to demonstrate good equality and diversity practice.

Adapting learning situations and resources

Being different (or perceived to be different) can mean being disadvantaged or being discriminated against by others. Advancing equality and promoting diversity is therefore the key to fostering a positive learning experience. The fact that one of your students might be different in some way is often based upon qualities or characteristics that cannot be changed. You therefore need to reduce barriers, challenge attitudes and behaviour, and include all students throughout your sessions. This can be achieved by adapting situations and resources, either before or during their use.

You might need to adapt various situations as they arise, for example if a discussion becomes biased, create an opportunity to discuss both sides of the argument. You might also have to adapt resources, for example to ensure a wide range of people are represented in handouts, or adapt something, for example a handout to make it accessible by all.

You will be in a good position to influence equality of opportunity by providing a learning environment that positively involves all your students, and is free from favouritism and discrimination, where your students are treated with respect.

Reasonable adjustments

The Equality Act (2010) presents a challenge to all teachers. It requires you to anticipate the needs of disabled students and ensure that *reasonable adjustments* are in place to make sure that they are not placed at a substantial disadvantage when compared with a non-disabled student. Everyone in your organisation must take positive steps to ensure disabled students can fully participate in all activities and achieve their aspirations and ambitions with the same degree of dignity and choice as their peers. This will ensure suitable provision is anticipated and available, rather than the student having to *adapt* to the provision that is offered. Organisations and all their staff need to focus on the needs of individual students and be ready to be flexible in the way that they are organised and their programmes are structured.

Differentiated questioning can help support students, for example students for whom English is a second language may need longer to process information or need questions rephrasing.

The following table shows some ways in which *reasonable adjustments* could be sensibly anticipated to meet the needs of students.

Promotional materials	These should demonstrate the organisation's thoughtfulness about ways in which programme provision can take account of the needs of all students, including those who declare they have a disability. They should also be available in different formats to reach all potential students.
Information	This should be accessible to all. E-mail or the intranet/VLE might be an appropriate alternative to notice boards or leaflets. Signs and notices could be in different languages.
Equipment and the environment	These should take account of the needs of diverse users. For example, an adjustable height workstation would ensure access for any current and future students who use a wheelchair. Specialist ICT software or hardware could be used. Ramps could be used to ensure access. Refreshment and toilet areas should be accessible to all.

Programme resources	Handouts and presentations could be adapted to other formats to make them accessible to all, for example large print, use of coloured paper.
	Consider the appropriateness of the level of the language or jargon used in relation to the subject level.
	Ensure equipment is working and accessible.
Liaising with others	The responsibility for all adjustments which may be required should be shared. Where organisations such as the Careers Service work with your students, they would have to agree for their disclosure to be shared since the Equality Act gives providers the duty to comply with students' requests for confidentiality.
	Language interpreters might be required and/or staff who can lip read or use sign language.
Assessment	Find out what can be reasonably adjusted. If your programme is externally accredited the awarding organisation will have an *Access to Assessment* policy which will state what can be done. For example, if knowledge is being tested and not writing skills, questions could be asked and answered verbally.
Feedback and evaluations	Information should be obtained from all students to ensure current practices are responsive to their needs and help anticipate future students' requirements.
	Not all students are able to provide feedback in hard copy, therefore electronic questionnaires, recorded conversations, e-mail or mobile technology might be more appropriate.
Staff development	This should ensure staff are well informed about current policies, and the types of needs of students, in time for that knowledge to be meaningful and have an impact.
	Ensure that disability equality is viewed as a shared responsibility by all staff.

When you are devising and planning your programme delivery, it is important to think about what it is that you expect your students to be able to do in order for them to be successful in their learning, and to consider the question: *what if (for whatever reason) they can't do that?* You may want to think about anticipating the likelihood that you will not be able to predict all reasonable adjustments. However, you should plan ahead to anticipate the likely adjustments required by disabled students, considering a full range of impairment types.

Example

David attends a local community centre where he is enrolled on a Confidence Building programme. The classroom is upstairs and as David is a wheelchair user he can only access this via the lift. On the morning of his third session he received a telephone call from the teacher to tell him that the lift was broken and the class had been moved to another room on the ground floor so that he could still attend. David was informed that all other students on the programme had also been contacted.

In this case the organisation and the teacher were proactive in making alternative arrangements and informed David before he arrived at the centre. This avoided an embarrassing situation for David and the other students in the very public reception area. Always try to anticipate the needs of your students and adapt any situations or resources as required. Know who to refer to for additional support (internally and externally) when queries or situations arise which you have not previously experienced.

Differentiation

Differentiation is about using a range of different approaches and resources to meet the needs of individuals and groups. It is very rare for a teacher to have a group of students who are all at the same level of ability, have the same prior knowledge and experience, and the same needs. You don't have to individualise everything you do; you just need to take individual needs into account, for example students' learning styles. You wouldn't help your students if you delivered a theoretical session to a practical group of students. Small group work is a good way to use differentiation. You could group your students for different activities by their learning style, level of ability, level of qualification or learning outcomes, past experiences or current knowledge, etc.

> *Differentiation can be defined as an approach to teaching and learning that both recognises the individuality of learners and also informs ways of planning for learning and teaching that take these individualities into consideration.*

> (Tummons, 2010: 93)

You could plan activities which *all* your students are capable of achieving, as well as some activities that *most* or *some* can achieve according to their level and ability.

Example

Paolo has a mixed group of level 2 and level 3 students. He knows the full group will be able to answer questions based on the level 2 syllabus, most will be able to answer from both levels and some will be able to answer questions based on the level 3 syllabus. He has therefore devised and used a differentiated questioning technique for his group of students.

Acknowledging and embracing the diverse nature of your students' age, experience, culture and background should help you include all students and bring your subject to life. Some students may work more quickly than others; giving them an extension activity could help develop and challenge their learning further without compromising the learning of others.

Activity

What will you need to know about your students to plan for effective differentiation of teaching, learning and assessment? How can you differentiate the objectives and resources to take into account the needs of your students?

If you can encourage your students to let you know of anything that you can do to help them, you will improve their learning experience. Simply asking, *Is there anything I can do to help your learning?* should ascertain this. Alternatively, ask yourself, *What can I do to give everyone a good learning experience?*

Differentiating your teaching, learning and assessment approaches should lead to more confident students who feel included, are motivated to learn and able to achieve. While it may take longer to plan and prepare your sessions to differentiate effectively, you will find your students are more engaged and motivated rather than being bored and uninterested.

Extension Activity

Evaluate how effective your organisation is in responding to student feedback regarding how they feel they are welcomed and how safe they feel within the first few weeks of attendance. How many students drop out within these first few weeks? Are they contacted to find out why and if so, how long does this take? How does your organisation manage and respond to the reasons why students leave? What can you do to prevent students leaving? What difference might it make to the individual student and the organisation?

Developing strategies for dealing with discrimination

Discrimination is about treating a person or group differently, often in a negative manner, usually as a result of prejudice or ignorance. It is about people being thought of as having different worth or value, being given fewer opportunities or being treated differently. However, not all differential treatment is discriminatory. Discrimination occurs when differential treatment cannot be objectively and reasonably justified.

The Equality Act (2010) prohibits discrimination on a wide range of grounds including nine protected characteristics:

- age
- disability
- gender
- gender identity
- marriage and civil partnership
- maternity and pregnancy
- race
- religion and belief
- sexual orientation

Example

A prospective student made enquiries about learning to speak English at her local college. She obtained some information and advice about the programme from the receptionist. As part of this procedure she was asked if she had resided in the country for more than three years, for the purposes of funding. The student asked if everyone who made enquiries about programmes were asked this same question or if it was only asked of certain groups or students.

Sometimes discriminatory assumptions are made about people as in this example, i.e. that some students might not be able to pay and may not be eligible for public funding for their learning. Reception and front line staff should not make assumptions from the way a person looks or speaks about whether or not they are eligible for public funding. In other cases, discrimination arises because people have decided that some people deserve to be treated less well than others.

Under the Equality Act (2010), there are seven different *types of discrimination*. An example of each of the following can be found in Chapter 1.

1. Associative discrimination: direct discrimination against someone because they are associated with another person with a protected characteristic.

2. Direct discrimination: discrimination because of a protected characteristic.

3. Indirect discrimination: when a rule or policy which applies to everyone can disadvantage a person with a protected characteristic.

4. Discrimination by perception: direct discrimination against someone because others think they have a protected characteristic.

5. Harassment: behaviour deemed offensive by the recipient.

6. Harassment by a third party: the harassment of staff or others by people not directly employed by an organisation, such as an external consultant or visitor.

7. Victimisation: discrimination against someone because they made or supported a complaint under equality legislation.

Activity

Have you ever been discriminated against in any way? How did this feel? Have you seen any of your students being discriminated against through any of the seven types of discrimination? If so, what did you do and would you do it differently next time?

Direct and indirect discrimination

Direct discrimination is where a person is less favourably or unfairly treated because they have a protected characteristic. This often arises because of assumptions, stereotyping, fear, ignorance or prejudice. This tends to be obvious discrimination.

Example

Jolene requests an extension for a piece of written work, and tells her teacher that the reason is that she is affected by medication for schizophrenia. Her teacher doesn't consider this a valid reason and declines the request. This is likely to be direct discrimination. The teacher cannot argue that it was not his intention to discriminate; the law only considers the end effect.

Direct discrimination also covers association discrimination or perception discrimination. This is direct discrimination against someone because they associate with a person who has the protected characteristic or because they are perceived to have a protected characteristic.

Example

Holly sees Ali, a Bangladeshi student, being subjected to racially abusive language and complains that this has caused her learning environment to be offensive, even though she is white and not the subject of the abuse.

Indirect discrimination occurs where a rule, requirement or condition appears to be fair because it applies equally to everyone, but in fact cannot be objectively justified because it can be shown to put people who share a protected characteristic at a much greater disadvantage than others.

Example

John responded to an advertisement for a catering teacher and was asked at interview if he would be prepared to be clean shaven (he has a beard) giving the reason as hygiene. This request therefore puts some religious groups at a disadvantage.

Positive action

Positive action can be classed as a set of measures to prevent or overcome past discrimination or to redress the balance of workforce representation. It can relate to any initiative aimed at people from under-represented groups. In some instances, positive action is permitted by equality legislation, i.e. where it is designed to redress perceived injustice. Positive action includes any activity that helps:

- address disadvantages experienced by students who share a protected characteristic

- meet the needs of students who share a protected characteristic, when these needs are different from those who don't share a protected characteristic

- address disproportionately low participation in learning

Example

An organisation has decided not to charge any fees for childcare for adult students who reside in identified disadvantaged communities. This targets students who by nature of where they live are already in a situation of inequality. This therefore advances equality of opportunity by reaching out to groups of people with low skills, who are not currently involved in learning and with a background of low income or disadvantage.

The Equality Act (2010) widened the scope of positive action so that when employers are in a situation where two candidates are equally qualified, the employer can choose to recruit the person from an under-represented group. Employers must still select on the basis of merit, and must not select a less qualified candidate who is from an under-represented group. The decision to appoint a person from an under-represented group when faced with two candidates of exactly the same merit is voluntary. Widening the scope of positive action in the Equality Act has the potential to help diversify the workforce. Misunderstandings about positive action can create problems. For example, instead of encouraging people to see the benefits of a diverse workforce, positive action could risk increasing suspicion of positive discrimination or political correctness.

Organisations should therefore ensure that everyone clearly understands what is meant by positive action and are not misinformed, for example by inaccurate media stories. They should also understand why positive action initiatives are taking place and not feel disadvantaged if they are not members of an under-represented group.

If at any time your students feel that discrimination has taken place then there are some sensible positive action steps to adopt:

- clarify the problem or concern with them

- complain within the organisation

- complain to an external person or organisation

- seek help and advice

- try to resolve the issue informally

- take legal action if applicable

- report it to the police, depending upon the severity of the incident

Students should be able to pursue this process without fear of recrimination. Bullying is also a form of harassment and may constitute a hate incident or crime. If any form of discrimination or harassment takes place it is stressful and intimidating for the victim.

Activity

Research direct and indirect discrimination further. Use the internet and other sources of information. In your experience so far can you think of any instances when you have witnessed any situations? What happened and how was it resolved?

Although pregnancy and maternity are not covered by indirect discrimination, policy and practice that disadvantages pregnant women and new mothers could constitute indirect gender discrimination.

Tactics for averting discriminatory behaviour

When considering forms of discrimination and harassment, it is important to bear in mind that different people have different cultural and social perceptions as to what they consider to be hostile or degrading. Some tactics you can use include using an appropriate icebreaker that everyone can participate in. Discussing and agreeing ground rules at the beginning of your programme, and keeping these on display, can help remind your students how to behave towards others. During an organisation's recruitment and selection process teachers are often asked what they understand by *equality and diversity* and how they ensure it in their teaching. Very often the response is that they would *treat everyone the same.* However, diversity, fairness and equality are about *treating others how* **they** *would wish to be treated,* rather than making assumptions on their behalf. Your students are all different and therefore have different needs and different degrees of need which will lead to equal outcomes at the end of their programme.

If possible, plan and facilitate a session with your students to try to address these different perceptions or assumptions. Ask your students what they consider discrimination is and discuss the differences between direct and indirect discrimination. You could carry out role play activities to demonstrate the differences. Inviting guest speakers from different cultures, religions and beliefs to talk about their experiences will help your students see things from another perspective.

Language

Language has a fundamental role to play in treating people fairly. This is not language as in English, Welsh, Polish, etc. but the words you use and the way you express them. You should give a clear message to all your students that you and your organisation value diversity and respect individual differences. Carefully examining the language you use and the way you use it will help ensure that you treat your students as individuals and not merely as members of a group. Communication is not just about words, however, and you should also ensure that your tone of voice, demeanour and body language convey the same message of inclusiveness.

Example

Gemma has been asked to plan, design and deliver a four-week 'Job Skills Programme for the Unemployed'. The students are referred to the programme from JobCentrePlus and the aim of the project is to prepare people who are unemployed to return to work. The very title of this project typecasts these students into a particular group. They are immediately identified as being without employment. Gemma therefore asks for the title to be changed from 'Job Skills Programme for the Unemployed' to 'Returning to Work'.

There are many diverse people who find themselves unemployed due to different circumstances, for example redundancy or a career break. The language used for the title of a programme can therefore affect who will apply for it. In this example it is positive action in favour of the unemployed. However, the content will be based around *returning to work* and could easily be adapted to suit others, and the mix of students will help promote inclusion and equality.

Activity

Consider the content of a programme you plan to teach. Think about the language you will use in your documents and resources, for example session plans, individual learning plans, progress records, teaching materials and resources. Do you think you would use any language which might stereotype or discriminate, or suggest you may prejudge people or groups in negative terms? Have you made up your mind about the group of students before you have met the individuals? Can you think of any other groups who may also be subject to this same stereotyping due to the nature of the programme they will be taking?

To genuinely demonstrate respect, understanding and fairness and tackle discrimination and exclusion, the language used needs to be consistent with those intentions. This means not only avoiding words and phrases that offend, but also using language which is inclusive of others. Everyone in your organisation should respect the views and feelings of others, and use language that neither offends nor excludes, intentionally or otherwise. You could research terminology which is broadly acceptable and which promotes best practice and professionalism, and share this with your colleagues. You need to think about the language you use and whether or not you unintentionally cause offence.

> *If we are truly to demonstrate respect, understanding and fairness, tackle discrimination and exclusion, we need to ensure that the language we use is consistent with those intentions.*

(Trades Union Congress, 2009: 2)

Language should not stereotype in any way. However, assumptions often occur such as *immigrants don't take the time to learn English but take the jobs that British people should have.*

Examples of other groups of students who might be subjected to language stereotyping include:

- disaffected young people
- lone parents
- long-term unemployed
- offenders (ex or current)

- older people

- people with mental health problems

- travellers

Driving forces for equality and diversity

When providing a student-centred approach that makes the specific learning needs of *all* students the starting point, organisations need to be flexible in their approach to the services offered to their students. They also need to know what the forces are that are driving equality and diversity, for example:

- legislation, which is regularly updated or amended

- significant change in the ethnic makeup of the population, resulting in the need for a greater awareness of differing needs

- greater expectations of services delivered by organisations, particularly in the public sector

- significant events followed by reports and recommendations that raise public awareness and highlight the need for change

To address all aspects of equality and diversity, organisations need to be aware of any potential situations and how they might impact on the services they provide. Training should be available to all staff to ensure they are up to date with relevant legislation as well as the organisation's policies and procedures.

Example

Jayne teaches at a Community Learning Centre and has a student who has asked for a private place to pray at a specific time during the programme. With the student's permission Jayne approached the Centre Manager and booked a room for the same time each week so that the student had some privacy for prayer at the time requested. Jayne discussed with the student options for catching up with the work missed while he was away from the programme delivery.

On this occasion Jayne was able to negotiate with the Centre Manager for a private room for her student. Fortunately at this time a room was available but this may not always be the case. Due to legislation, the organisation must make a *reasonable adjustment*; however, it might not always be possible to respond to every need in this way.

The following are some ways in which you can drive equality and diversity.

- Being respectful to the needs of people from different races and cultures, even when this might cause a negative impact within the group.

- Challenging the negative impact.

- Being genuine in your desire to be fair, and remaining professional at all times.

- Being sensitive and respectful to the thoughts, feelings and opinions of others.

- Demonstrating your knowledge and commitment to advancing equality and diversity, creating a positive atmosphere of trust and respect and improving outcomes for all your students.

- Raising awareness within the group of the differences between people, and being aware of the impact of behaviour upon others.

- Showing empathy by putting yourself in the other person's position and imagining how they might think and feel in the circumstances, then looking back at your own behaviour from their perspective.

- Thinking through the consequences of actions to stop you or your students making a prejudicial comment that might offend someone.

- Valuing the experiences of others, and incorporating this into your sessions.

Think of equality and diversity as being an extension of the skills and knowledge that you already have and use during your teaching and learning sessions. Planning ahead will help reduce any potential occurrences of discrimination and dealing with situations as they arise will help change attitudes and demonstrate that you are proactive rather than reactive.

Extension Activity

When planning your next session with students, what changes can you make to your resources to ensure they are inclusive and do not include any stereotyped images or references? Can you include a discussion with your students based on a recent event, perhaps in the national or regional news, which explores equality and diversity and is also relevant to your subject?

When delivering your session, ensure you include everyone in the group and use their name. After the session, evaluate how you communicated and behaved with your students. What would you now do differently?

Summary

In this chapter you have learnt about:

- demonstrating good practice

- adapting learning situations and resources

- developing strategies for dealing with discrimination

Cross-referencing grid

This chapter contributes towards the following: scope (S), knowledge (K) and practice (P) aspects of the Professional Teaching Standards (A–F domains) and the Equality and Diversity assessment criteria at levels 3 and 4. Full details of the learning outcomes and assessment criteria for the units can be found in the appendices.

Domain	Standards
A	AS3, AS5, AS6, AS7; AK3.1, AP3.1, AK5.2, AP5.2, AK6.1, AP 6.1, AK6.2, AP6.2, AK7.1, AP7.1, AK7.2, AP7.2
B	BS1, BS2, BS3, BS4, BS5, BK1.2, BP1.2, BK2.1, BP2.1, BK2.5, BP2.5, BK3.4, BP3.4, BK4.1, BP4.1, BK5.2, BP5.2
C	CS1, CS3, CK1.2, CP1.2, CK3.2, CP3.2
D	DS1, DS2, DK1.1, DP1.1, DK1.3, DP1.3, DK2.1, DP2.1, DK2.2, DP2.2
E	ES1, ES2, ES3, ES4, EK1.2, EP1.2, EK2.1, EP2.1, EK2.4, EP2.4, EK3.1, EP3.1, EK3.2, EP3.2, EK4.1, EP4.1
F	FS1, FS4, FK1.1, FP1.1, FK1.2, FP1.2, FK4.1, FP4.1, FK4.2, FP4.2
Equality and Diversity unit	**Assessment criteria**
Level 3	1.1, 1.2, 1.3, 2.1, 2.2, 2.3, 3.1, 3.2, 3.3, 4.1, 4.2, 5.1
Level 4	1.1, 1.2, 1.3, 2.1, 2.2, 2.3, 3.1, 3.2, 3.3, 4.1, 4.2, 5.1

Theory focus

References and further information

Ayers, H and Gray, F (2006) *An A to Z Practical Guide to Learning Difficulties.* London: David Fulton Publishers

Clements, P and Spinks, T (2000) *The Equal Opportunities Handbook: How to Deal with Everyday Issues of Unfairness.* London: Kogan Page

Government Equalities Office (2011) *Equality Act 2010: Public Sector Equality Duty What do I need to know? A Quick Start Guide for Public Sector Organisations.* Crown Copyright

IODA (2010) *Diversity, Fairness and Equality Information Booklet.* Tadcaster: IODA Limited

Rose, C (2010) *The New Equality Act: What does it mean for the Further Education and Skills Sector?* Coventry: Learning and Skills Improvement Service (LSIS)

Tomlinson, J (1996) *Inclusive Learning.* Further Education Funding Council/ HMSO

Trades Union Congress (2009) *Diversity in Diction, Equality in Action – A Guide to the Appropriate Use of Language.* South West TUC; also available at www.swan.ac.uk/media/media,30840,en.pdf [accessed 03.01.12]

Tummons, J (2010) *Becoming a professional tutor in the Lifelong Learning Sector* (2nd edn). Exeter: Learning Matters

Wallace, S (2007) *Managing Behaviour in the Lifelong Learning Sector* (2nd edn). Exeter: Learning Matters

Websites

CIPD – www.cipd.co.uk/hr-resources/guides/managing-diversity.aspx

Equality Act (2010) – www.legislation.gov.uk/ukpga/2010/15/contents

Equality and Human Rights Commission – www.equalityhumanrights.com

Excellence Gateway – tlp.excellencegateway.org.uk/tlp/pedagogy/equalityanddive/index.html

Home Office – www.equalities.gov.uk

Institute for Learning – www.ifl.ac.uk

National Learner Panel – www.excellencegateway.org.uk/pdf/NLP%20 Ofsted%20SES.pdf

Ofsted – www.ofsted.gov.uk/resources/handbook-for-inspection-of-further-education-and-skills-september-2009

4 HELPING AND SUPPORTING OTHERS

Introduction

In this chapter you will learn about:

- identifying Inequality
- identifying barriers to inclusion
- supporting equality and diversity

There are activities and examples which will help you reflect on the above and assist your understanding of how to help and support others. At the end of each section is an extension activity to stretch and challenge your learning further.

At the end of the chapter, there is a cross-referencing grid showing how the content of this chapter contributes towards the Professional Teaching Standards and the Equality and Diversity assessment criteria at levels 3 and 4. There is also a theory focus with relevant references, further information and websites you might like to refer to.

Identifying inequality

When teaching, you will want to be fair and treat all your students equally, but may be concerned that you, or another student, will say or do something that will offend or upset someone. You will need to identify forms of inequality in your teaching and in your organisation to alleviate any negative impact this might have. Forms of inequality are broader than those covered by the protected characteristics of equality, and can be divided into two dimensions:

Primary: Characteristics which are inherent or quite noticeable	Secondary: Characteristics which are less obvious or less noticeable
Age	Ability and intelligence/skills
Attitude	Criminal record
Colour	Disability – mental
Culture	Education
Disability – physical	Employment status
Dress	Family background and status
Ethnicity	Financial status
Gender	Gender identity
Language, accent, dialect	Gender reassignment
Physical appearance	Health (permanent or temporary)
Sexuality	Home environment
	Marriage and civil partnership
	Maternity and pregnancy (early stages)
	Nationality
	Political conviction
	Race
	Religion or belief
	Sexual orientation

The table lists characteristics against which many people show prejudice and therefore may be the target for discriminatory practices. There are far more secondary than primary characteristics so it is important never to assume anything, but to base the characteristics on fact.

Activity

Look at the table above and consider what other characteristics could be added to each column. Could any occur in both columns? If so why? Do you feel you have ever been unfair to an individual or group because of one or more of the characteristics? Always ask yourself how you would like to be treated to ensure you are fair to everyone.

As a teacher you will need to be aware of the legislation that will impact on you and your organisation's relationship with your students. You will also need to be aware of how you relate to the primary and secondary dimensions, particularly those in the secondary category which are less obvious or noticeable. Sometimes prejudices can be innate and you need to reflect on your own attitudes, values and beliefs and subsequent behaviours, and whether or not your students are affected by this.

Example

Bernie is the Arts and Design Curriculum Manager for an Adult Community Learning Service. He has been asked to organise a Creative Arts programme for a group of young people who are not in employment, education or training (NEET). He has asked for a volunteer from his teaching staff to deliver the programme but no one comes forward. Bernie talks to some of the teachers about this and they say they don't want to teach in disadvantaged areas with young people who have issues or problems.

This example shows how some dimensions, i.e. age, criminal records, education, family background and home environment, can relate to preconceived ideas about certain groups, which may be ill-informed. In the advert, these young people were identified as NEET, leading Bernie's staff to make certain assumptions. This form of inequality can result in difficulties in recruiting teachers to work with these particular groups, which can exacerbate feelings of social exclusion among young people who are NEET.

Activity

Can you think of a time when you have turned down an offer of teaching or were apprehensive about teaching a group because you have had preconceived ideas about what the students would be like? If so, have you learnt from this experience not to have preconceived prejudice?

Environments

Every person is a unique individual, but each develops in a social setting in which they are influenced by, and interact with, other people. The attitudes and values people have in regard to their surroundings greatly affect interactions between the person, society, culture and the environment, which will have an impact on their capacity to learn. Environments present societies with both opportunities and restraints. One of the government's priorities for post-16 learning is to increase participation in areas of high deprivation. If you are required to teach in community settings in this environment then you will need to be aware of the forms of inequality and discrimination that some of your students might have or are currently experiencing. If the individual or group you are teaching knows that people have made negative assumptions or have preconceived ideas about them, they will expect to be treated in a particular way because they are perceived to be different. This can make teaching them difficult. The impact on your students may be a lack of self-confidence and self-esteem, or demotivation, resulting in an unwillingness to try new things and/or poor social skills.

Example

A group of ten young unemployed single mums from a disadvantaged area identified an interest in working in an office. The training manager at the children's centre they attend has asked your organisation to provide a one-week Communication Skills programme on their premises. At the first session the students expected to be treated as they were when they were at school and behaved accordingly, for example throwing things at each other and talking over you.

At school, some of these students behaved in this way for various reasons and expected their first learning experience as adults to be the same as at school. They were perhaps nervous and defensive about the whole experience, which caused them to act the way they did.

Activity

Looking at the previous example, what would you have done to manage these disruptions and ensure the learning experience was effective and positive for these students?

You might have thought about using a suitable icebreaker to help the students get to know each other and you better, and then following this by agreeing some ground rules. This would help establish a starting point for learning to take place more effectively. You would need to treat each person as an individual, encouraging their learning and development, and helping them realise that the fact they are single mothers is irrelevant and they are people in their own right. Being a single mother is just one aspect of them as individuals and does not wholly define them.

Extension Activity

Keep a diary for a few weeks and make an entry every time you see or hear an action that undermines the ethos of equality and diversity. This could be during your teaching sessions, when communicating with colleagues or witnessing local or national events. What strategies could you use or suggest to make sure they don't occur again in the future?

Identifying barriers to inclusion

Inclusion recognises every individual's right to be treated equally, and to be accorded the same access to products, services and opportunities as everyone else. It is the state of being *included*. Many people face particular barriers in taking up the opportunities society has to offer; these are known as *barriers to inclusion*. Often these are associated with particular groups, for example families or pensioners, who are more vulnerable to poverty, or those who are subject to discrimination or disadvantage for reasons of gender, race or disability. Other barriers are more personal and can be directly damaging to an individual's prospects of inclusion, for example poor health, homelessness or drug misuse. Other barriers might be as simple as a lack of affordable local childcare or transport.

The following list includes some of the barriers and challenges your students might experience which would make them feel excluded and that learning opportunities are not within their reach:

- access to childcare
- access to or fear of technology
- access to the location and learning environment
- age
- bullied in the past
- costs too high
- culture and language differences
- different or specific learning needs
- emotional or psychological problems
- ethnicity/race/faith/religion

- family problems or commitments
- fear of embarrassment
- fear of joining a group
- financial reasons
- having to attend on their own
- hearing or visual impairment
- hyperactivity
- inappropriate learning environment
- inequality, i.e. stereotyped gender roles
- lack of confidence, motivation, social skills
- lack of resources
- lack of support at work to be allowed time to attend learning
- learning difficulties and disabilities
- limited basic skills such as literacy, numeracy and ICT
- medical reasons
- peer pressure
- personal/work/home circumstances
- physical, medical, mental or health problems
- poor childhood experiences of learning
- preconceived negative feelings/ideas
- returning to an educational environment after a long break
- shift work
- shyness and lack of confidence or self-esteem
- specific needs or requirements
- transient populations (for example gypsies)
- transport difficulties
- type of teaching, for example e-learning might not be appropriate

You may feel you can deal with some of these yourself; however, you should always refer your students to an appropriate specialist or agency if you can't deal with them. Never feel you have to solve any student problems yourself and don't get personally involved; always remain professional.

You may encounter students with varying degrees of needs; therefore you should remain impartial, but sensitive. If a student discloses something to you which is covered by the Equality Act (2010) the whole organisation is deemed to know. It is therefore important that any issues are communicated to all concerned, and acted upon.

Example

Dave informed his teacher that he is dyslexic and asked if any handouts could be printed on cream paper. He also asked if anyone minded if he used a digital recorder during the sessions, as he preferred to listen to this afterwards rather than make notes. His teacher asked the group if they were all happy to have handouts on cream paper and whether they minded Dave recording the session. All the group agreed to his requests. The teacher also informed a colleague who taught Dave to ensure they were being consistent with their support.

You should always refer your students to an appropriate specialist or agency if you can't deal with their needs. Never feel you have to solve any student problems yourself and don't get personally involved. You will need to find out who or what is available internally within your organisation or where you could seek advice or refer students externally.

Situations are very real for your students where barriers and challenges are linked to practical issues, for example access to childcare, emotional issues, problems at home or a lack of self-confidence.

Activity

Make a list of people and organisations who you could seek advice from, or refer your students to. Having this information accessible along with contact details will help you when it's needed.

The image your organisation, and indeed you as a teacher, portrays, can have an effect upon whether your students decide to attend a programme with you or not.

Example

Xuxia teaches a textiles programme. Her students have been in her class for two terms, developing their skills and knowledge, and working on individual projects. As they have been together so long, they all know each other, and Xuxia very well. A new student joins the group at the start of the next term; she only stays for three sessions and then doesn't return.

Inclusion means allowing people into a group, i.e. excluding no one. In this example the form of inequality is that of an individual joining a majority group. The new student perhaps felt uncomfortable joining a well established group which was familiar with the teacher, the programme, the environment and the norms in the classroom. Most new students would find this situation difficult, therefore there is immediately a risk factor involved in retaining this student in that they are likely to feel excluded. You may have students who join your programme later than others. Always make them feel welcome, introduce them to the others to help them belong, and ensure you help them catch up with what they have missed. You could also pair them up with someone in the group so they don't feel alone.

Activity

Can you think of a time during your teaching when a student has not stayed beyond the first few sessions? Did you find out why the student decided not to return? Was it something that could have been anticipated and successfully dealt with?

If this has happened in the past, try to find out why. You may be able to encourage your student to come back again, perhaps by talking to them outside of the learning environment by telephone.

Your organisation's Equality and Diversity Policy should include promises to your students, for example to:

- actively work against a culture of dependency
- ensure that individuals are valued in their achievements and progression opportunities are recognised
- place the student at the centre of the learning process
- practise a philosophy of equity as opposed to exclusivity

- provide a curriculum and support that is relevant to each student

- provide an inclusive learning environment to ensure that reasonable adjustments can be made for the learning needs of as wide a cross-section of the general population and local community as possible

- take into account the diverse range of support needed to enable individuals to participate and learn, and utilise any learning aids or adaptations to resources

At each stage of their learning journey talk to your students and ask them what works best for them, for example what they find difficult and what has worked for them in the past. Some learning difficulties and disabilities come with labels, for example *Asperger's syndrome*, and this may lead to you making assumptions about what you think you need to do to support this student's learning. The brain of individuals with adult Asperger's syndrome works in a different way, especially when it comes down to *processing information*. Their focus is on details and they mostly specialise in one field of interest. Asperger's symptoms in adults can stabilise over time and this provides them with opportunities to improve their social skills and behaviour. There are impairments in social interaction like maintaining friendships or feeling the need to engage in activities with others, and in communication such as taking whatever is said literally and being unable to read between the lines.

By talking to your students, you can find out if there are any areas you can help and support them with. Never assume you know what's best for them.

Example

Musnah has declared on her enrolment form that she has dyspraxia. For some students they may need to move around the room frequently. This may not be the case with Musnah – you will only find out how to teach her effectively by discussing with her what support she needs.

Try to develop individual strategies for your students and don't make assumptions about any learning difficulties or disabilities they may declare to you. This could lead to the nature of the difficulty being misunderstood and to inappropriate treatment, i.e. bullying or isolation. Being uncomfortable when approaching and managing students with learning difficulties or disabilities can be more about your embarrassment than theirs. All your students will want to take advantage of the same opportunities as other students, and to feel like an accepted member of the group.

Activity

Imagine you are teaching a Card Making programme. You have been advised that a student who is deaf has enrolled on your programme and will be supported by a sign language interpreter. What will you need to consider when preparing to teach this programme?

You would need to think about how you might adjust your own teaching style to suit that of the student, and how you might design and organise individual and group activities to ensure that everyone understands what they are to do, and can take part. You will need to create and present resources so that everyone can use and read them, whether or not you need any special equipment. Where an interpreter is needed, ensure there is room for the interpreter to sit by the student, and that the student who needs to lip-read can see everything you demonstrate, as well as seeing others in the group.

When involving others in the learning process, you need to:

- decide who needs to know what and when, to maintain good communications with your colleagues

- discuss roles and responsibilities with your colleagues at the start of your joint working relationship – where other professionals such as sign language interpreters are involved, they will have their own code of conduct and will be able to brief you about this

- discuss where support workers will position themselves in the room during various activities, to ensure that students can participate fully and safely

- explain the plan for each session to any student support assistants, sign language interpreters and bi-lingual interpreters so that they can explain the key points to students; they may need guidance on this if they are not familiar with your subject

- make arrangements to have materials translated into the appropriate medium well before the session, to accommodate students with literacy and language needs, or a visual impairment

- make sure that all colleagues understand the principles of safe working and do not present any obstacles during the session

- set out a clear code of conduct for student support workers so that they support their students without interfering with the progress of the session

- well before the session, show student support workers any written or visual materials you will use so that they can brief students effectively

People you may need to communicate with, besides your students, are those who are internal and external to your organisation.

Internal	External
administrators	careers advisors
assessors	employers
colleagues	external quality assurers
exam officers	inspectors and regulators
internal quality assurers	others involved in the teaching and
invigilators	assessment of your students
managers	parents, guardians or carers
mentors	prison officers
student support workers	probation officers
support staff	social workers
teachers	staff from other organisations and
trainers	agencies

Remember that if a student has informed you of something that could affect their learning, you are obliged to communicate with others to ensure a consistent approach to support their needs.

Try to capture all of your intentions on your scheme of work and session plans. These are working documents for all those involved in the learning experience and are good evidence of embedding equality and diversity if you need to provide it to inspectors. It is good practice to plan ways in which students can work together at some point during your sessions, while having their individual needs met at other times.

Working with agencies

There is a need for transformational change in the Lifelong Learning Sector, for example regional and local inter-agency collaboration. This is good practice and should be built upon and extended to enable an increased choice of high quality adult provision appropriate to your students' assessed needs. This should take into account students with learning difficulties and/or disabilities and be student-centred and cost effective in the use of public funds. It should also enable students to progress to the maximum possible level of independence and activity in their communities and employment.

Example

Janine delivers and assesses the Level 2 Certificate in Working with Children and Young People at her local training centre. The curriculum team has planned for someone from the LSCB to deliver the knowledge outcomes on child protection.

This good practice is an example of inter-agency collaboration and inviting experts who are occupationally competent in a particular field to deliver specialist parts of the programme.

Single Equality Scheme

In moving towards meeting the challenges set out in the Leitch Review of Skills (2006: 9), the SFA has developed a *Single Equality Scheme (SES)* which is designed to place equality and diversity at the heart of what they do, i.e. through high quality education they can create a more socially cohesive society. Current evidence suggests that raising the skills of under-represented and under-achieving groups could have a significant impact on economic growth. According to the National Skills Forum (2010), raising the employment rate of disabled people to the national average could boost the UK economy by £13 billion. Geoff Russell, Chief Executive of the SFA states:

> *We are committed to placing equality and diversity at the heart of what we do. There is a direct correlation between skills, productivity and employment. Only by eliminating discrimination and embracing diversity can we ensure that every single person is able to take advantage of the opportunities available to them and make a valuable contribution to the economic success of this country.*

> (http://skillsfundingagency.bis.gov.uk/news/pressreleases/ SES+consultation.htm (accessed 25.10.11))

The SFA Single Equality Scheme is a framework by which they will work to implement the new equality duties that were set out in the Equality Act 2010. It takes account of the existing equality duties (race, gender and disability), as well as the new protected characteristics (sexual orientation, religion and belief, age, gender identity, maternity and pregnancy). This means that the SFA will challenge all their providers to measure outcomes for students in relation to equality and diversity against the priorities they have set.

These priorities are:

- communities feel that they have a reasonable chance of success
- employers able to compete in a global economy
- increased recognition of the value of vocational qualifications
- more adults getting relevant skills
- more young people succeeding
- provision that is relevant to the future
- qualifications that are recognised and valued in the workplace
- improving job outcomes
- raising participation

The Single Equality Scheme sets out the SFA's response to their duties and commitment to promoting equality and diversity which then shapes their priorities. This is then translated into targets for their providers, i.e. your organisation if you receive funding, and then yourself and how they relate to your students and the programmes you are teaching.

Activity

Consider the priorities in the bulleted list above set out by the SFA for the purposes of funding. Can you relate these to the programme(s) you teach? Do you think that your programme(s) fit these priorities? If not, what could be changed?

Where funding is streamlined and particularly focused on very specific priorities your organisation should be considering the curriculum it offers. It might be that certain programmes will no longer be offered if they do not meet with the funding priorities. It is important for you to be aware of the priorities and to keep up to date with new programmes and developments in your specialist area.

Education plays an important role in helping your students achieve their potential in life. For some, it can give new opportunities and stop them being trapped in a life of disadvantage. It is therefore important that everybody has access to appropriate educational opportunities.

Recognising the contribution of diversity within society requires everyone to respect other individuals, and to treat them fairly and with dignity. Without respect and good relations between groups, your students may not be able to take an active part in decisions that affect them, and they may be prevented from accessing and fulfilling their potential. A lack of respect between students from different backgrounds can also contribute to social unrest. Students should have the opportunity to express their views and beliefs freely, while respecting those of other students.

Activity

Your organisation should have systems and structures to support all students to successfully complete their learning programme. Find out what these are and how they can be communicated to and accessed by your students. Incorporate these into your planning and delivery process.

Grievances, complaints, and appeals

At some point during the teaching and learning process, one of your students may have a grievance, a complaint or even wish to appeal against one of your decisions. They will need to know who they can go to, and that the issue will be followed up. You may also have a grievance yourself and need to know what to do. Organisations should have relevant policies and procedures in place; a policy states *what* the organisation's commitment is, a procedure states *how* the policy will be implemented. There may be separate policies and procedures for staff and for students, which may be available in handbooks, given during induction, on a notice board, or available via your organisation's intranet. Make sure you are familiar with these; they will usually be reviewed yearly, and should be dated to ensure their currency.

Activity

Locate your organisation's policies and procedures for grievances, complaints and appeals (for staff and for students). See when these were last reviewed and who is responsible for them. Do you know what to do if a student makes a complaint?

You may have found there is one policy for all three aspects, with separate procedures for staff and students. Familiarising yourself with them will ensure you know what to do in case any problems do arise.

An organisational positive and proactive culture towards equality and diversity should help reduce the numbers of grievances, complaints and appeals. This can be achieved by all staff within the organisation taking issues seriously and partaking in training to increase awareness. You also need to know that your own behaviour can impact on your organisation's culture. Being negative may only breed negativity among others; being positive should influence others to be positive too.

Sometimes students may have a grievance, but not bring this to your attention for fear of it being seen as an over-reaction, or that the issue might become worse as a result and they might be discriminated against. It's important to watch what's happening during your sessions. If you see a student is withdrawn, or doesn't want to sit next to someone or work with a particular student, have an informal chat with them to see if you can help in any way.

Grievances and complaints can often be dealt with informally, without the perpetrators knowing. However, if you feel a problem is more serious, your organisation's procedure should always be followed, as legal rights may be lost if it is not.

Example

Greg is a teacher at your organisation, and confides in you that he is gay. He tells you he feels he didn't get a promotion because of this and has therefore been discriminated against. You encourage him to follow the organisation's complaints procedure, but he doesn't want to make a fuss. You tell him that it doesn't have to be him that makes the complaint, but that you could raise a grievance about discrimination within the organisation. He doesn't want you to do this either. It could be that Greg didn't get the promotion because of his ability, not because he is gay. Greg should really have an informal chat with his manager to gain some feedback regarding his interview. He can then decide whether his complaint is valid, if it is, following the organisation's procedure will ensure everything is documented, in case a tribunal is involved at some stage in the future.

If you raise a grievance about discrimination, it is against the law for your organisation to treat you badly as a result, as this is victimisation, whether it relates to you, or to someone else. It is also against the law to be treated badly for supporting someone else's complaint about discrimination, for example by giving evidence to support their grievance.

The grievance or complaints procedure should not be used in retaliation because you are annoyed with something someone has done or said. If you feel that you have been unfairly treated, and your complaint is genuine, then don't wait too long. Anyone following up your complaint will wonder why you hadn't complained about it before, and that could weaken your case. The same will apply to your students. If you feel they have a valid complaint, encourage them to follow the procedure; don't wait for things to get worse if you can't resolve the issue informally.

Example

Student Grievance and Complaints Procedure

Any grievance or complaint should be made in writing to the Student Services Manager, clearly setting out the problem. A written response will be made within seven days, along with an invitation to a meeting to discuss the problem. A parent, carer or other representative may be present at the meeting. Within a further seven days, a written decision will be made. An appeal can be made against this decision within 14 days.

Some organisations will provide a pro-forma for students to use for their grievance or complaint, which ensures all the required details are obtained. Others might encourage an informal discussion prior to a formal complaint. Statistics should be maintained regarding all grievances and complaints. These will help the organisation when reviewing their policies and procedures. An anonymous *suggestion box* can often be a way to encourage students to express their concerns in confidence. This way, your organisation can be *proactive* regarding potential problems, rather than being *reactive* afterwards.

Students should be encouraged to have a voice via the quality systems in place, for example to give feedback as part of an evaluation questionnaire. Additional questions or opportunities for comments should be combined with standard questions about teaching and learning. This will give students the opportunity to share their views on issues that relate directly to them and their needs in the learning environment. Ideally you will have already addressed their needs through open and frank discussions. However, obtaining feedback will help you address any concerns.

Harassment and bullying

Harassment is any behaviour deemed offensive by the recipient. Students can claim they find something offensive even when it's not directed at them. Organisations are also potentially liable for the harassment of their staff and students by people they don't directly employ, for example employers and contractors.

The Equality Act (2010) applies equally to the harassment of heterosexual people as it does to the harassment of lesbians, gay men and bisexual people. Organisations may be held responsible for the actions of their staff as well as the staff being individually responsible. If harassment takes place in the workplace or at a time and place associated with the workplace, for example a work-related social gathering, the organisation may be liable and may be ordered to pay compensation unless it can be shown that it took reasonable steps to prevent harassment. Individuals who harass might also be ordered to pay compensation.

The Equality Act does not specifically cover harassment on the grounds of pregnancy and maternity, or marriage and civil partnerships. However, direct discrimination prohibits treatment such as bullying or harassment that results in a person being treated less favourably than others.

Setting ground rules at the commencement of a programme can help promote a climate of respect among students, ensuring boundaries are set and followed by all. Role play activities can be a way to bring an awareness of harassment and bullying to your group. During tutorial sessions with your students, you could note any problems on your tutorial forms; this would ensure a formal record was kept in case it was needed in the future.

Most organisations now have a policy for harassment and bullying. Find out if there is one available for your students, and ensure they are aware of it.

Example

Harassment and Bullying Policy

This organisation is committed to promoting a positive environment where all staff and students can expect to be treated with dignity and respect. Staff and students have the right to work in a climate free from harassment and bullying. If an issue cannot be dealt with informally, the grievance and complaints procedure should be followed. All complaints will be taken seriously and investigated fully, with appropriate action being taken as a result.

Examples of harassment and bullying include:

- derogatory or rude comments
- display or circulation of offensive materials or books
- ignoring others
- undermining someone's confidence
- intrusive questioning about ethnic origin, race, belief, etc.
- name calling, verbal abuse or taunting
- offensive or insulting jokes or literature
- physical or mental abuse
- racist and/or sexist comments or jokes
- unfair allocation of work
- unnecessary references to sex
- unwanted physical contact

As a result of harassment and bullying, morale can be lowered, stress, anxiety and harm can be caused, and ill health and poor performance can occur. Harassment is a disciplinary offence and may be illegal. You might be able to deal with some problems informally. However, if you have any cause for concern, always take this further before it gets out of control. Once you have reported a problem, your organisation must follow this up and do all they reasonably can to put a stop to it.

As part of your teaching role, you may be assessing your students, marking tests and assignments, etc. Your judgements may affect your students' future career prospects. They therefore have a right to appeal against your decision, and your organisation should have a student appeals procedure, outlining the stages involved. The appeals procedure should be available to students when they commence the programme and you should familiarise yourself with it.

Example

Student Appeals Procedure

Stage one – within seven days of receiving the assessment decision, discuss the issue with the assessor concerned, to clarify the reasons for the grade.

Stage two – if the issue has not been resolved, put this in writing to the Internal Quality Assurer (IQA), or Programme Manager, within seven days. This may result in a re-assessment of your work. A response will be made within 14 days.
Stage three – if the issue has still not been resolved, put this in writing to the Student Services Manager within seven days, who will respond within 14 days.
Stage four – if you are still not happy, you can request your appeal be heard by the Appeals Panel at their next meeting, who may inform the awarding body responsible for your qualification. Their decision will be final.

If the programme you teach and assess is externally quality assured, i.e. a representative from the awarding organisation visits to ensure compliance with their regulations, they will ask to see records of any appeals. They may also talk to your students to ensure they have received a fair learning and assessment process.

Example

Cheryl was working towards a Level 3 Certificate in Hairdressing. She had been observed in the workplace by her supervisor, who had said she wasn't yet competent at one of the units, but Cheryl felt she was. When the External Quality Assurer (EQA) visited, he asked her if she had registered a formal appeal. Cheryl said she hadn't, but had discussed it with her assessor at the college, who had arranged to go into her workplace to carry out an observation the following week. The EQA clarified this with the assessor, who confirmed Cheryl's supervisor was not a qualified assessor and could not make the final decision.

If any of your students do have a grievance, complaint or appeal, this should not affect the way you, other students or staff treat them. You should always remain professional in your role, to promote a positive learning environment.

Extension Activity

Your organisation will be working with many diverse groups of people, both staff and students, and they will all be affected by organisational policies. Find out if your organisation has carried out an equality impact assessment regarding its grievances, complaints and appeals procedures.

If your organisation has done so, then evaluate the impact this assessment has had on any policy reviews. If not, then find out who in your organisation is responsible for these assessments and discuss how you can contribute to an equality impact assessment being carried out to ascertain whether or not the procedures fairly address the needs of all students.

Supporting equality and diversity

To support equality and diversity you need a positive attitude and the ability to be proactive. You should deal with any issues of harassment, discrimination, stereotyping or bullying which might occur within your sessions.

Harassment includes behaviour that is offensive, frightening or in any way distressing. Your students can claim something is offensive even when it is not directed at them. There might be intentional bullying which is obvious or violent, but it can also be unintentional, subtle and dangerous. It might involve nicknames, teasing, name-calling or other behaviour which is not with malicious intent but which is upsetting or hurtful. It might be about the individual's sexual orientation (real or perceived) or it may be about the sexual orientation (real or perceived) of those with whom the individual associates. It might not be targeted at an individual but consist of a general culture which, for example, appears to tolerate the telling of homophobic jokes.

To help take reasonable steps to overcome any problems you should:

- know about your organisation's policies and procedures for dealing with your students' complaints, which should have been shared with students during induction – the policy should explain:

  - a definition of unacceptable behaviour

  - how students can report bullying, harassment or any other forms of unacceptable behaviour

  - how you and the organisation will deal with unacceptable behaviour

- treat all complaints seriously, regardless of who brings them, and investigate the complaint thoroughly

- deal quickly and firmly with anyone who acts inappropriately

- deal with matters informally and internally if possible – the solution may be as simple as pointing out to a student the effect that their behaviour has on others and asking them to stop

- be consistent, open and fair in all decisions

If you have the opportunity, hold a group discussion to help break down any assumptions. As you interact with others of different cultures, there is no good substitute for receptiveness to interpersonal feedback, good observation skills, effective questions and some common sense. There is much to be gained by observing how people of the same culture interact with each other. Don't be afraid to ask questions as most people respond very positively to enquiries about their culture. Ask a variety of people to obtain a balanced view and challenge any stereotyping as it occurs.

If you can make a genuine effort to find the positive historical, literary and cultural contributions of a society, learn a few polite expressions in another person's language, and show appreciation for the food and music of another culture, you can have positive effects upon that person.

Verbal and non-verbal communication

In everyday conversation, spoken words are only one way to communicate. As little as seven per cent of a message may be expressed in words. The rest is through facial expression, voice tone, body gestures and overall posture. When the verbal and non-verbal messages don't match up, people often pay more attention to the non-verbal message.

It can be easy to misunderstand non-verbal messages because different cultures have different expectations about eye contact, physical touch, body gestures, etc. A person's gender, age, position in society and individual preference can complicate communication even more.

Culture greatly influences attitudes about physical contact, whether it's a handshake, hug, or pat on the back. In Asia, female friends often hold hands and men casually embrace one another as they walk along the street. In other cultures, for example in America, people may feel uncomfortable with such public behaviour. In some cultures, affectionately patting an adult's head is strictly taboo, and pointing with fingers or feet is not acceptable.

How close should people stand to each other when they're having a conversation? In areas of the Middle East and South America, people stand very close when talking. European Americans like to have more distance between them, while some African Americans prefer even more space. You can create great discomfort by standing too close to another person. Not being aware of this can even prevent someone from understanding or accepting the ideas you're trying to convey.

To create a positive environment for communication, your non-verbal message must closely match your verbal message. First, recognise your own expectations about non-verbal communication, and then find ways to learn about those of individuals and other cultures. One way to do this is to carefully observe how people and families speak and behave around each other and with people of authority. This can provide clues about the true meaning of their non-verbal interactions.

Non-verbal messages have a powerful impact on what's communicated. When a person is sensitive to these silent messages, they are far more likely to interact with others in a friendly, comfortable manner and to make the spoken message more understandable.

Differences between cultures and people are real and can add richness (and humour) to your learning programme. People everywhere have much in common, such as a need for affiliation and love, participation and contribution. When the exterior is peeled away, there are not so many differences after all. Students need to know that they will be comfortable and safe, and that the environment is suitable for their needs.

Example

The local college provides a separate common room for Muslim students, as well as a prayer room for staff and students. Food to meet the specific cultural and religious dietary requirements of the community is also provided. There are signs and posters in community languages which are openly displayed.

All learning environments should be welcoming by promoting a multicultural, inclusive ethos, regardless of the ethnic profile of their staff, students or the local community. This is imperative for organisations with a public commitment to inclusive learning and widening participation. More welcoming messages and positive visual images might be needed. Examples of promoting diversity might include positive and diverse images of students, multi-faith prayer rooms, and catering facilities with a varied menu for a range of dietary requirements. Where possible the availability of diverse social facilities for students is vital as a means of developing and spreading good practice. The development of diverse curricula and policies for the student, and the value of opportunities provided to work with like-minded groups is key to embracing and supporting equality and diversity within the learning environment.

Motivation

Maslow (1987) introduced a *Hierarchy of Needs* in 1960 after rejecting the idea that human behaviour was determined by childhood events. He felt that obstacles should be removed that prevent a person from achieving their goals. He argued there are five *needs* which represent different levels of motivation which must be met. The highest level was labelled *self-actualisation*, meaning people are fully functional, possess a healthy personality, and take responsibility for themselves and their actions. He also believed that people should be able to move through these needs to the highest level provided they are given an education that promotes growth. It could be that some of your students are hungry or thirsty when they attend your session, or feel threatened by others. If you can help meet their needs through the different levels, they will be able to aim towards achieving their desired outcomes.

The following figure shows the needs expressed as they might relate to learning, starting at the base of the pyramid with the first level needs.

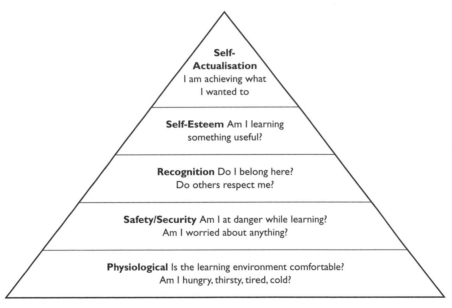

Figure 4.1 Maslow's (1987) Hierarchy of Needs expressed in educational terms

Extension Activity

Look at Maslow's Hierarchy of Needs and state how you could ensure that each level can be achieved by your students. Research the needs further at www.businessballs.com/maslow.htm and by reading relevant texts.

Summary

In this chapter you have learnt about:

- identifying inequality
- identifying barriers to inclusion
- supporting equality and diversity

Cross-referencing grid

This chapter contributes towards the following: scope (S), knowledge (K) and practice (P) aspects of the Professional Teaching Standards (A–F domains) and the Equality and Diversity assessment criteria at levels 3 and 4. Full details of the learning outcomes and assessment criteria for the units can be found in the appendices.

Domain	Standards
A	AS1, AS2, AS3, AS4, AS5, AS6, AS7, AK1.1, AK2.1, AK2.2, AK3.1, AK4.2, AK4.3, AK5.1, AK5.2, AK6.1, AK6.2, AK7.1, AP1.1, AP2.1, AP2.2, AP3.1, AP5.1, AP5.2, AP6.1, AP6.2, AP7.1
B	BS1, BS2, BS3, BS4, BS5, BK1.1, BK1.2, BK1.3, BK2.1, BK2.2, BK2.3, BK2.5, BK3.1, BK3.2, BK3.3, BK3.4, BK4.1, BK5.1, BK5.2, BP1.1, BP1.2, BP1.3, BP2.1, BP2.2, BP2.3, BP2.4, BP2.5, BP3.4, BP3.5, BP4.1, BP5.1, BP5.2
C	CS2, CS4, CK1.2, CK2.1, CK3.2, CK3.3, CK3.4, CK3.5, CP1.2, CP2.1, CP3.2, CP3.3, CP3.4, CP3.5, CP4.2
D	DS1, DK1.1, DK2.1, DK2.2, DP1.1, DP1.3, DP2.1, DP2.2
E	ES2, ES3, EK2.1, EK3.1, EK3.2, EP2.1, EP3.1, EP3.2
F	FS1, FS4, FK1.1, FP1.1, FK1.2, FP1.2, FK4.1, FP4.1, FK4.2, FP4.2
Equality and Diversity unit	Assessment criteria
Level 3	1.1, 1.2, 2.1, 2.2, 2.3, 3.1, 3.2, 3.4, 4.1, 4.2, 5.1, 5.2
Level 4	1.1, 1.2, 2.1, 2.2, 2.3, 3.1, 3.2, 3.4, 4.1, 4.2, 5.1, 5.2

Theory focus

References and further information

Clements, P and Spinks, T (2000) *The Equal Opportunities Handbook*. London: Kogan Page Limited

IODA (2010) *Diversity Fairness and Equality Information Booklet*. Tadcaster: IODA Limited

Leitch, S (2006) *The Leitch Review of Skills. Prosperity for all in the global economy: world class skills*. Final Report. London: HMSO

Maslow, AH (1987) *Edited by Frager R Motivation and Personality* (3rd revised edn). New York: Pearson Education Ltd

National Skills Forum (2010) *Doing things differently: step changes in skills and inclusion*. London: National Skills Forum

Skills Funding Agency (2010) *Single Equality Scheme: Our Strategy for Equality and Diversity*. Coventry: Skills Funding Agency

Websites

Equality and Human Rights Commission (EHRC) – www.equalityhumanrights.com

Great Schools: How Cultural Differences May Affect Student Performance – www.greatschools.org/special-education/support/704-cultural-differences-student-performance.gs

Human Rights Act (1998) – http://tinyurl.com/tmqq9

NIACE – www.niace.org.uk/current-work/area/mental-health

Project Implicit – https://implicit.harvard.edu/implicit/research/

Quality Improvement Agency: Improving teaching and learning – www.qiaresources4adultlearning.net/

Skills Funding Agency – www.skillsfundingagency.bis.gov.uk

5 REVIEWING YOUR OWN CONTRIBUTION

In this chapter you will learn about:

- interacting with others
- sources of information and external agencies
- evaluating own practice

Introduction

There are activities and examples which will help you reflect on the above and assist your understanding of how to review your own contribution towards advancing equality and diversity in the learning environment. At the end of each section is an extension activity to stretch and challenge your learning further.

At the end of the chapter, there is a cross-referencing grid showing how the content of this chapter contributes towards the Professional Teaching Standards and the Equality and Diversity assessment criteria at levels 3 and 4. There is also a theory focus with relevant references, further information and websites you might like to refer to.

Interacting with others

It is important to interact with others, both internal and external to your organisation, to ensure you are being fair to your students and colleagues. During the student interview or induction stages of your programme, you should find out any particular requirements or needs of your students. If you happen to cover a class for someone else, under the Equality Act (2010), the whole organisation is *deemed to know* about any student requirements that have been disclosed. If this information has not been communicated to you, it is wise to ask your students if there is anything you need to know to help or support them. You might like to encourage your students to talk to you at the break time or after the session, rather than cause any embarrassment in front of their peers.

Activity

Explore the needs of your current students if you haven't already done so. If there is something that others in your organisation should know in order to provide better support or a better service, discuss this with them. Ensure that you undertake this in a sensitive way, to enable them to support your students too.

It's always wise to ask your students how you can help them, as you must never assume what they need and they might not want to discuss their concerns in front of others.

You need to be aware of students' competence regarding basic skills such as literacy and numeracy as well as those students:

- with different learning styles

- for whom English is not their first language

- requiring privacy, for example for prayer, or for medical needs

- who are partially deaf or sighted

- who do not eat during the daylight hours of Ramadan

- who do not want to eat meat, or certain foods, for religious or other reasons

- who may have to leave early as they have dependants or caring responsibilities

- who may not be able to attend all sessions due to work patterns

- with a physical, mental or learning difficulty, for example Asperger's syndrome, autistic spectrum disorder, etc.

- with dyslexia, dyspraxia, dysgraphia or dyscalculia

- who may experience financial difficulties

Finding out anything that may affect your students or the learning process prior to commencing your sessions will help you plan more effectively.

Taking into account your students' needs and ensuring you embrace equality and diversity will help to deliver an inclusive session. You may need to liaise with staff within your teaching team or organisation who can give support to your students. This support could be to help improve skills, for example literacy and numeracy, or to help students who are partially sighted or deaf, or who have any other additional requirements. You need to work within the boundaries of your teaching role; don't try to address any issues yourself that you are not confident or experienced with. There should be staff within your organisation who you could approach to advise you on the support arrangements available.

Example points of referral include:

Internal	External
careers advisers	awarding organisations
counsellors	banks or building societies
examination officers	bereavement counsellors
financial services staff	carers
first aiders	charities
health and welfare officers	childcare agencies
initial advice and guidance staff	Citizens Advice Bureaux
interpreters	health centres and general
student support staff	practitioners
mentors	hospitals
student union representatives	Job Centre Plus
	motoring and transport organisations
	police
	Samaritans telephone helplines and
	agencies such as: abuse, alcohol,
	Childline, Crimestoppers, debt,
	drug, Lesbian and Gay switchboard,
	gambling, NHS Direct, Parentline,
	victim support
	Weight Watchers

There may be other issues you need to deal with, for example stereotyping, prejudice and discrimination. Witnessing an incident during your session gives you the chance to challenge it as a naturally occurring opportunity. If you see anything taking place within your sessions, or hear of anything that could disrupt your sessions, you need to deal with this in a sensitive manner, otherwise the affected student might lose confidence, not participate during activities or even leave the programme as a result. Communication is the key, not only between you and your students, but among the group. During the induction stage of your programme, it would be good practice to include a session on the concepts of equality and diversity, highlighting how stereotyping, prejudice and discrimination can affect individuals and groups, and stressing the importance of taking individual responsibility and action to help and support others. This will form a good basis for the beginning of your programme, contribute to the negotiation and setting of ground rules, and hopefully filter through to the students' home, community, and workplace to improve other relationships. Students will gain increased knowledge, experience and skills from others in the group; they will also feel a sense of acceptance and belonging, and gain respect from others. Fostering respect between all students will ensure that students from minority groups are not treated any differently from any other group.

Your behaviour can help influence change within your organisation, and that of your students. Ways to demonstrate positive behaviour include:

- being fair and consistent with assessment decisions

- being sympathetic or empathic to students' problems

- challenging students' own attitudes, values and beliefs

- encouraging and supporting students to make the best use of their abilities

- following all legal requirements

- following all organisational policies and codes of practice

- making time available to talk to students about any concerns

- taking an active interest in students' interests or problems

- treating individuals with dignity and respect

- using a range of activities and resources to promote inclusivity within your sessions

When communicating, try to use words which support equality and diversity, and encourage your students to use them too, to prevent any unfair labelling. Words used to describe people can cause offence even if they are considered to be acceptable descriptions, for example visually challenged in place of blind. Everybody has their own preferences and will have a term or phrase to describe themselves. Talking to your students will give you the information you need.

Activity

Consider your reactions to incidents which have occurred with your students, for example comments, labels or actions which are not acceptable. Describe what occurred, how you challenged it and what you could do differently next time.

Scale of Prejudice

A model regarding *unfair treatment* is Allport's (1954) *Scale of Prejudice and Discrimination*. It was devised by psychologist Gordon Allport and shows what happens if unfair treatment is not stopped.

Allport's Scale of Prejudice goes from 1–5:

1. antilocution (name calling, stereotyping)

2. avoidance (defamation by omission, exclusion)

3. discrimination (refusal of service, denial of opportunity)

4. physical attack (threat of physical violence, murder)

5. extermination (mass assassination, genocide)

Examples of these are as follows.

1. Antilocution – a majority group freely makes jokes about a minority group. Speech is in terms of negative stereotypes and negative images, also called hate speech, and is commonly seen as harmless by the majority. Antilocution itself may not be harmful, but it sets the stage for more severe outlets for prejudice.

2. Avoidance – people in a minority group are actively avoided or ignored by members of the majority group. No direct harm may be intended, but harm is done through isolation.

3. Discrimination – a minority group is discriminated against by denying them opportunities and services that the majority group have, putting prejudice into action. Behaviours have the specific goal of harming the minority group by preventing them from achieving their goals. The majority group is actively trying to harm the minority.

4. Physical attack – the majority group vandalise the minority group's possessions or attack individuals, causing harm.

5 Extermination – the majority group seeks to eliminate or exterminate the minority group. When groups act out their prejudice with physical violence, the way is prepared for directing that energy methodically. In extreme circumstances this can lead to war.

You may experience some of these stages within your groups, perhaps to a lesser degree, or have witnessed things happening within the community or society where you live or work. They shouldn't be ignored. However, you may not feel experienced enough to deal with some issues, therefore you will need to seek the help of others in the early stages to avoid putting people at risk of harm.

Minority and majority groups

At some point you will have experienced equality and diversity issues within your teaching sessions as all your students are individuals and have different needs. As you become more experienced at recognising the needs and actions required, you will be able to incorporate these into your planning for your sessions. However, all your students will benefit from a discussion or a workshop and the setting of ground rules to increase their awareness. You will be familiar with the phrase *ethnic minority*. There will always be an *ethnic majority* where you teach. The demographic makeup of any country changes over time and you may teach in an area of the country where the majority of your students are immigrants, therefore the minority are those born in this country. Alternatively, you may teach in an area where the population may be small and therefore not very diverse. Where minority communities are not well represented on your programme, it is even more important to consider how to make your teaching more appealing and relevant.

Example

Linda had been asked to analyse some statistics regarding her groups of students for the past academic year. Besides retention and achievement, this includes gender, age range and ethnic minorities. Linda's organisation is based in a very small town, the only ethnic minority group was the family who owned and worked in the local Chinese restaurant. Her subject of Beauty Therapy tended to attract females who had recently left school. All of her students were female aged 16–19 and white. Her EQA had asked her what she was doing to recruit males and those from ethnic minority groups.

In this situation, it would be difficult for the organisation to recruit students from ethnic minority communities. A way of recruiting males could be by visiting the local school to promote the programme to both males and females, and producing leaflets and posters which included pictures of males as well as females. Positive imaging of males in the industry within the marketing materials might also encourage males onto your programmes.

If you feel your group does not represent society locally, regionally or nationally, this does not mean you are not differentiating for your students. You will have individuals who are all different in some way, for example a single mother who may need to arrange childcare, a student with dyslexia who prefers handouts on coloured paper, or a student who lacks confidence as they were bullied at school. Supporting your students with their individual requirements will help create an encouraging learning environment.

Some people may not have a positive attitude, or be prepared to challenge their own or others' attitudes, values and beliefs. People might try to justify their actions without basing these on facts, or may have inherited negative attitudes. It may take time to change this, but, as a teacher, you can make a difference to people's lives by embracing the diverse nature of your students, encouraging their individuality and challenging negative situations in the classroom.

Extension Activity

How confident do you feel you are to challenge issues such as prejudice, discrimination, bullying, etc.? Make a list of who you could liaise with at your organisation in order to support your students or to deal with difficult situations. How can you contact them and how available are they when you might need them?

How do you feel your own behaviour and the organisation's culture impacts upon your students?

If you don't feel confident at dealing with situations, ask at your organisation for some training and guidance.

Sources of information and external agencies

Many organisations are dedicated to the promotion of equality and diversity, and produce useful information, books, leaflets, videos, magazines and other resources. Your own organisation should be proactive and have policies and procedures in place, with information available for staff and students. By now, you should have found out what is available to you, but you may need to research further for any specific information that could help you and your students.

The following are details of some of the many organisations that have useful information and/or resources regarding equality and diversity. Each has a website for further information.

- Advice, Conciliation and Arbitration Service – www.acas.org.uk – aims to improve organisations and working life through better employment relations. It helps with employment relations by supplying up-to-date information, independent advice and high quality training, and by working with employers and employees to solve problems and improve performance.

- Audit Commission – www.audit-commission.gov.uk – an independent watchdog, driving economy, efficiency and effectiveness in local public services to deliver better outcomes for everyone.

- British Broadcasting Corporation – www.bbc.co.uk/religion – provides a comprehensive section on religion and ethics.

- Centre for Equality and Diversity – www.cfed.org.uk – a registered charity promoting the interests of all black and minority communities.

- Chartered Institute of Personnel and Development – www.cipd.co.uk – the professional body for those involved in the management and development of people.

- Department for Business, Innovation and Skills (BIS) – www.bis.gov.uk – BIS is making a difference by supporting sustained growth and higher skills across the economy. Almost everything that BIS does – from investing in skills to making markets more dynamic and reducing regulation, and from promoting trade to boosting innovation and helping people start and grow a business – helps drive growth.

- Directgov – www.direct.gov.uk – easy access to information and public services from the UK government.

- Equality and Diversity Forum – www.edf.org.uk – a network of national organisations committed to progress on age, disability, gender, race, religion and belief, sexual orientation and broader equality and human rights issues. It was established in January 2002 to promote dialogue and understanding across the separate equality strands, and to ensure that policy debate on proposals for discrimination legislation and a single equality body recognises the cross-cutting nature of equality issues.

- Equality and Diversity UK – www.equalityanddiversity.co.uk – various resources for purchase, information, publications and statistics to improve understanding of issues relating to equality and diversity.

- Equality and Human Rights Commission – www.equalityhumanrights.com – champions equality and human rights for all, working to eliminate discrimination, reduce inequality, protect human rights and build good relations, ensuring that everyone has a fair chance to participate in society.

- Fire and Rescue Service – www.communities.gov.uk/fire/firerescue service/ – the *Equality and Diversity Strategy's* vision is to create, by 2018, a service which can demonstrate that it serves all communities equally to the highest standards, building on a closer and more effective relationship with the public and creating a more diverse workforce which better reflects the diversity of the local working population in each area.

- Government Equalities Office – www.homeoffice.gov.uk/equalities – responsible for the government's overall strategy and priorities on equality issues. This includes the Discrimination Law Review, the Single Equality Bill, and the Equality Public Service Agreement.

- Higher Education Funding Council for England – www.hefce.ac.uk – committed to promoting equality and diversity within the staff and student bodies in higher education.

- Local Government Improvement and Development – www.idea.gov.uk – supports improvement and innovation in local government. The Equalities and Cohesion team helps councils to build equality into their core business planning and respond positively to challenges that new legislation brings.

- Investors in People – www.investorsinpeople.co.uk – provides straightforward, proven frameworks for delivering business improvement through people. Information regarding key legislation, leading campaigners, business improvement and good practice tips regarding racial equality in the workplace are available on the site.

- Law Society of Scotland – www.lawscot.org.uk – the Society promotes the interests of the solicitor's profession in Scotland and the interests of the public in relation to the profession.

- Learning and Skills Improvement Service – www.excellencegateway.org.uk – an online portal for staff in the further education and skills sector with free resources to support teaching and learning.

- Liberty – www.liberty-human-rights.org.uk – Liberty is also known as the National Council for Civil Liberties. It was founded in 1934 as a cross-party, non-party membership organisation at the heart of the movement for fundamental rights and freedoms in the UK. Liberty promote the values of individual human dignity, equal treatment and fairness as the foundations of a democratic society. They campaign to protect basic rights and freedoms through the courts, in Parliament and in the wider community through a combination of public campaigning, test case litigation, parliamentary lobbying and policy analysis. They also provide free advice and information.

- MIND – www.mind.org.uk – a charity to advance the views, needs and ambitions of people with experience of mental distress, promote inclusion by challenging discrimination, influence policy through campaigning and education, and inspire the development of quality services which reflect expressed need and diversity.

- Ministry of Defence – www.mod.uk – useful information regarding equality and diversity in the Royal Navy, Royal Air Force and British Army.

- National Health Service – www.nhsemployers.org – equality and diversity are at the heart of the NHS strategy. NHS Employers' equality and diversity team offers advice, assistance and support to NHS organisations.

- National Institute of Adult Continuing Education – www.niace.org.uk – exists to encourage more and different adults to engage in learning of all kinds. It campaigns for and celebrates the achievements of adult students, young and old, and in all their diversity. NIACE is the largest organisation working to promote the interests of students and potential students in England and Wales.

- Pinnacle – http://pinnacletrainingsolutions.co.uk – is passionate about learning and embedding equality. Its rich and wide experience includes working within and in partnership with a range of organisations facing different challenges. Support is designed to be interactive; Pinnacle knows where the best resources are (including free ones) and can point you in the right direction.

- Police – www.homeoffice.gov.uk/police – all of the police-related information, support and guidance published by the Home Office, useful to all ranks of serving police officers and anyone involved in the world of policing and justice.

- Post Compulsory Education & Training Network – www.pcet.net – a dedicated, UK-based, further education website which has been designed to support further education teachers from all subject disciplines.

- Royal Mail Group – www.royalmailgroup.com – articles and reports, interviews and features to do with diversity at Royal Mail Group and beyond.

- Scottish Disability Training – www.sdt.ac.uk – free resources relating to equality and diversity, funded by the Scottish Funding Council (SFC) and based in the School of Computing at the University of Dundee.

- Skills Funding Agency – www.skillsfundingagency.bis.gov.uk – SFA is a partner organisation of the Department for Business, Innovation and Skills (BIS) and their job is to fund and regulate adult further education and skills training in England. Their mission is to ensure that people and businesses can access the skills training they need to succeed in playing their part in society and in growing England's economy. They do this in the context of policy set by BIS and informed by the needs of businesses, communities, and sector and industry bodies.

- Stonewall – www.stonewall.org.uk – equality and justice for lesbians, gay men and bisexuals.

- The British Council – www.britishcouncil.org – an international organisation working in over 100 different countries contending with complex equality and diversity issues.

- The Learning and Skills Network – www.lsnlearning.org.uk – an independent not-for-profit organisation committed to making a difference to education and training. It aims to deliver quality improvement and staff development programmes that support specific government initiatives, through research, training and consultancy, and by supplying services directly to schools, colleges and training organisations.

- The Royal Society – www.royalsociety.org – the UK's academy of science which seeks to play an important role in helping to ensure that the UK is maximising the opportunity for all of the population to contribute to the development of science, engineering and technology. The Royal Society believes that UK science would benefit from a more diverse and inclusive culture.

- The Working Group – www.theworkinggroup.org – a non-profit media company that combines television, internet and web resources in the areas of workplace issues; race, diversity and the battle against intolerance; and encouraging democracy and citizen participation.

- Times Educational Supplement online – www.tes.co.uk/resources – free resources produced by teachers for schools and post-16 students.

- UNICEF – www.unicef.org.uk – education resources and information.

Activity

Carry out a search via the internet for 'equality and diversity'. See what other organisations there are that you could access to gain further information and useful resources. You may be surprised at just how much information is available, from a wide variety of organisations, groups and associations.

If you come across any useful activities, try these out yourself, and if you feel they are appropriate, encourage your students to use them.

External agencies

There are other external agencies or people you will come into contact with as part of your teaching role. These include:

- careers advisors, Job Centre Plus staff

- employers, parents and carers

- external quality assurers from awarding organisations

- inspectors, for example from Ofsted

- schools, colleges, universities and training organisation staff

- stakeholders, for example funding bodies such as the YPLA and Local Education Authorities (LEAs), and partners, for example voluntary and community groups

Working with other agencies can help advance equality and diversity within your organisation. There may be experienced and knowledgeable people who are willing to come to your organisation and give talks to your students, or you could access them for information and resources, or just to help improve your knowledge. You could also encourage your students to partake in extra-curricular activities, for example joining local societies or clubs. There will also be events in your local area which your students may benefit from attending as their knowledge and understanding of particular groups will be advanced through attendance and involvement. This may include local Gay Pride events, multi-cultural festivals and/or religious celebrations.

Whenever you need to communicate with anyone outside of your organisation, remember that you are its representative, and your own attitude may be taken as an extension of the attitude of the organisation. Therefore, it is important to remain professional at all times.

The need for awareness extends beyond yourself, the teaching staff and your own students, to others who give support, for example caretakers, canteen staff, learning resource staff, volunteers, etc. The management of your organisation and relevant Boards of Governors should also be proactive in advancing equality and diversity. The recruitment, selection, teaching, support, assessment and review of students and staff should always be based on potential and ability.

Stephen Williams, Head of the Equality and Diversity Unit at the Advisory, Conciliation and Arbitration Service (ACAS), states:

> It must be an intolerable situation to know you are working in an environment where you feel your contributions are not valued. Unfortunately many can suffer – for years sometimes – without being able to overcome this problem, and even more worrying is that employers are not trained to be aware of the types of issues that can make people feel undervalued and ineffective.

(www.trainingreference.co.uk/news/el061108.htm [accessed 25.09.11])

This has been the main driver behind ACAS devising a series of equality and diversity e-learning tools designed to help organisations recognise relevant issues and be able to address them.

Extension Activity

Access www.acas.org.uk/elearning/ and register for the equality and diversity online e-learning tool. Complete the programmes which you consider are relevant to your teaching role.

Access the Equality and Diversity Forum at www.edf.org.uk and have a look at their information bank. See if there is anything useful you could use with your students and register for online updates.

Evaluating your own practice

When evaluating your own practice, you need to consider *how* your own behaviour has impacted upon your students. If you are proactive and have a positive approach, you may still need to challenge your own attitudes, values and beliefs to ensure you accept and respect others. Your organisation may have a culture of embracing equality and diversity issues, or it may not. If not, you may need to do something about this to ensure other staff, as well as you yourself, are treating all students with respect and understanding.

Activity

Think about the way you act with your students. Answer the following questions honestly, and then consider carefully how you could address any negative responses.

- *Do you use eye contact with all your students?*

- *Do you have a favourite student whom you give more attention?*

- *Do you ask questions to everyone in the group, or just a few?*

- *Do you discriminate in any way – directly or indirectly?*

- *Do you make any prejudicial or offensive comments towards any students?*

- *Do you ignore or embarrass students for any reason?*

- *Do you touch your students in a way that could be construed as inappropriate?*

- *Do you ensure your teaching methods and resources are accessible to all your students?*

Perhaps you used a handout which didn't reflect different cultures, or a student had difficulty understanding some jargon you had used. You might have had a student with a physical difficulty who struggled to access some equipment, or couldn't take part in an activity. You might have a student who really excels, and you subconsciously give them more praise and encouragement than others. You might even have wanted to impose your own values and beliefs on others, for example if you didn't agree with something a student said. If you felt there were some issues, try to plan ahead in future to create a more inclusive environment for all your students. You could use the checklist in Appendix 5 to help you with your planning and teaching.

Activity

Think about what has contributed to your own attitudes, values and beliefs. Have you managed to formulate your own opinions regarding equality and diversity, or do you feel you have been influenced by others, the organisation within which you work, or your family, community and society.

Various factors may have contributed, for example your upbringing and home life, the country you have lived in, the community in which you live, attitudes of parents or guardians, the influence of colleagues, the culture at previous organisations, or friends and family. You need to realise what has influenced you to help you make your own opinions, and to consider and respect others. Various issues will arise during your sessions; there will be different interactions between yourself and your students, and between the students in your group, which may create awkward situations. Being proactive and developing an understanding of the differences of your students is much better than being reactive to a situation after it has happened. If you feel the problems have arisen due to a lack of knowledge on the part of your students, you could carry out an *awareness raising* session with your group to help them realise the impact that equality and diversity has on others. If you felt you hadn't prepared adequately, or had an issue that you couldn't satisfactorily resolve, it might be an idea to seek out a relevant training opportunity. It is possible your organisation will encourage its staff to embrace equality and diversity issues and provide regular training, or you may be able to attend a programme elsewhere. Your organisation might have an appraisal process, and this would be a good opportunity for you to discuss any areas you don't feel confident with, in order to improve. You might also receive feedback from your line manager or others within your organisation, who may observe your sessions to ensure you are teaching effectively and being inclusive. External inspectors or awarding organisation personnel may also observe your teaching or assessment practice to ensure you are being fair to all students. If you receive any negative feedback, don't take this personally, but look at *why* this was, and ask *what* you could do to improve for the future.

Example

Aisha is a part-time teacher, covering for an absent member of staff for six weeks. She has a group of students who are taking a cookery programme and is being observed by her manager. During the session, she asked the group to plan a main meal for four people of either roast beef or roast pork with vegetables and potatoes, which they would cook during the next week's session. Two students in the group looked at each other and mumbled, but didn't say anything to Aisha. Throughout the remainder of the session, they whispered among themselves but Aisha didn't challenge this, even though it became disruptive to the others. During the manager's feedback to Aisha, he asked her if any of her students had religious beliefs which would impact on the session or were vegetarian, to which Aisha replied she didn't know. He recommended she follow this up with her students, and take further training to help improve her knowledge. He also recommended she deal with any disruption when it arises, and offer alternative menu choices to ensure all students would be included.

Continuing professional development

There are constant changes in education; therefore it is crucial to keep up to date with any developments. Examples include changes to the qualifications you will teach, changes to policies and practices within your organisation, regulatory requirements and government policies. Your organisation may have a strategy for CPD which will prioritise activities they consider are important to improving standards. CPD can be formal or informal, planned well in advance or be opportunistic, but should have a real impact upon your teaching role, leading to an improvement in practice.

If you are working towards ATLS or QTLS, you must evidence your CPD annually. Once you have achieved your ATLS or QTLS status, you will need to maintain your Licence to Practise by partaking in relevant CPD activities, which the IfL will monitor and sample.

Opportunities for professional development include:

- attending events and training programmes

- attending meetings

- e-learning activities

- evaluating feedback from peers and students

- improving own skills such as literacy, numeracy and ICT

- membership of professional associations or committees

- observing colleagues

- researching developments or changes to your subject and/or relevant legislation

- secondments

- self-reflection

- shadowing colleagues

- standardisation activities

- studying for relevant qualifications

- subscribing to and reading relevant journals and websites

- visiting other organisations

- voluntary work

- work experience placements

- writing or reviewing books and articles.

All CPD activities must be documented in some way and reflected upon. This can be via the IfL website, your organisation's systems, or your own manual or electronic record. Maintaining your CPD will ensure you are not only competent at your job role, but also up to date with the latest developments.

Attending training events should be a part of your CPD. Taking the Equality and Diversity unit of the Professional Teaching Qualifications will contribute towards your CPD, as well as improving your knowledge and skills.

Activity

Think about the areas you feel you need to develop regarding equality and diversity. Consider any training needs you might have, and how you could address these. Follow this up by talking to someone at your organisation who could help, perhaps your mentor or someone from the human resources department.

There is continual change in our population, the European Union is growing, and there are major global transformations taking place; you therefore need to keep up to date with changes and developments. There is often debate about what it means to be *British*, which focuses on religion, culture-related beliefs and dress, and this can impact on learning and community cohesion. Legislation needs to be followed, as well as your organisation's own policies and procedures; you therefore need to ensure your knowledge and practice remain current.

Self-evaluation

Self-evaluation is a good way of continually reflecting upon your own practice to ensure you are carrying out your role effectively. When evaluating your own practice, you need to consider how your own behaviour has impacted upon others and what you could do to improve.

A straightforward method of reflection is to have an **E**xperience, then **D**escribe it, **A**nalyse it and **R**evise it (EDAR). This method incorporates the *who, what, when, where, why* and *how* (WWWWWH) approach and should help you consider ways of changing and/or improving.

Experience → Describe → Analyse → Revise (EDAR)

- Experience – a significant event or incident you would like to change or improve.

- Describe – aspects such as who was involved, what happened, when it happened and where it happened.

- Analyse – consider the experience more deeply and ask yourself how it happened and why it happened.

- Revise – think about how you would do it differently if it happened again and then try this out if you have the opportunity.

Reflection should become a habit, for example mentally running through the EDAR points after a significant event. As you become more experienced and analytical with reflective practice, you will progress from thoughts of *I didn't do that very well*, to aspects of more significance such as *why* you didn't do it very well and *how* you could change something as a result. You may realise you need further training or support in some areas therefore partaking in relevant CPD should help.

There are various theories regarding reflection, Schön (1983) suggests two methods:

- reflection in action
- reflection on action

Reflection *in action* happens at the time of the incident, is often unconscious and allows immediate changes to take place. It is about being *reactive* to a situation and dealing with it straight away.

Reflection *on action* takes place after the incident and is a more conscious process. This allows you time to think about the incident, consider a different approach, or to talk to others about it before making changes. It is about being *proactive* and considering measures to prevent the situation happening again in the future.

Example

Ian was teaching a group of Motor Vehicle students. There were 11 males and one female – Iman. He had ignored previous taunts by a group of four males towards Iman and had actually laughed at one of their jokes. However, today he noticed Iman was visibly upset and had been excluded from a group activity. Ian immediately went over to her to find out why. He then spoke to the others and diffused the situation to enable Iman to join the group. This was 'reflection in action'. Normally, he would have ignored the situation and just thought afterwards about what he could have done differently, i.e. 'reflection on action'. The latter would not have helped Iman during the current session.

Part of reflection is about knowing what you need to change. If you are not aware of something that needs changing, you will continue as you are until something serious occurs. Maintaining your CPD and keeping up to date with developments in your subject area, changes in legislation, changes in qualification standards and developments with ICT will assist your knowledge and practice. If you haven't already done so, joining a professional association like the IfL will give you lots of benefits as well as access to resources and events.

Activity

Reflect upon the last session you taught using EDAR to help you. Did you experience any issues, for example discrimination, stereotyping or prejudice? If you did, what could you do to stop this happening again? Were there any naturally occurring opportunities that you managed to embed within your session? If so, what worked well?

You may see your own skills developing, for example becoming more diplomatic, sensitive, tolerant and respectful to others. Evaluating yourself, your teaching and your group's learning will help to improve your practice in the future. You might identify issues or problems that can be overcome regarding equality and diversity, for example by producing handouts with different font sizes or colours, not using gender bias when talking, and moving furniture to make areas accessible. However, be careful not to overdo things by meeting the needs of the minority to the detriment of the majority.

Obtaining feedback

Feedback from students is always useful to help you evaluate your teaching and your group's learning. Encouraging students to talk to you about anything you can do to help them, or things you can change to support their learning, will help build a climate of trust and respect. Never make assumptions that the programme is going well, just because you think it is. Students may be embarrassed to talk in front of their peers, but unless you know of any issues that may affect them, you can't fully support them.

> *Creating opportunities for learners to provide meaningful feedback is a fundamental part of a learner involvement strategy. It helps to shape the services offered to learners. In the context of the expert learner, learner voice activities are more specifically focused on involving learners in evaluating their experiences of learning, and in providing feedback on what works for them. Involving them in this way helps to develop their awareness of how they learn best and of what they need to do in order to achieve their goals.*

(http://tlp.excellencegateway.org.uk/tlp/xcurricula/el/learnervoice/ whatisthelearne/index.html (accessed 21.10.11))

The *Learner Voice* is about involvement of students and potential students in shaping the learning opportunities that are available to them. It means involving students in reforming the lifelong learning system at all levels by supporting them to act as partners with policy makers, providers, practitioners and other agencies. Learner Voice initiatives enable students to express their views, needs and concerns and also ensure that organisations respond appropriately to the issues that they raise. The policy emphasis on putting students *at the heart of the system* has increased in recent years. A range of policy initiatives to strengthen the Learner Voice have been introduced, including:

- organisational student involvement strategies
- greater focus on the *learner* voice in Ofsted inspections
- a national student panel

Activity

How creative and innovative is your organisation at involving students at all levels and at making decisions about policies and procedures? Can you suggest ways in which this could be improved?

Questionnaires

Besides encouraging informal feedback and discussions, you can gain formal feedback from your students by issuing questionnaires. Your organisation may have standard ones you are required to use, or you could design your own.

When designing questionnaires, you need to be careful about the type of questions you are using, and consider why you are asking them. Don't just ask questions for the sake of issuing a questionnaire; consider what you really want to find out. When writing questions, gauge the language and complexity to suit your students, and the types of responses you require to aid analysis. Will your questions be closed, i.e. a question only requiring a *yes* or *no* answer; will they be multiple choice, enabling the student to choose one or more responses to a question; or will they be open, leading to detailed responses? Questions eliciting responses which can be totalled up are known as *quantitative*; those eliciting a detailed response are known as *qualitative*. Whichever way you gain responses and feedback, make sure you do something with them, to help improve your practice and the support you give your students.

Example

Did you receive an individual learning plan? YES/NO

This is a closed question and would not help you to understand what it was that your student experienced, and they might just choose 'yes' to be polite. It would, however, be easy to add up the number of 'yes' and 'no' responses to gain *quantitative data*. The questions would be better rephrased as open questions to encourage students to answer in detail. This would provide you with *qualitative data*, therefore giving you more information to act on.

Example

How detailed was your individual learning plan?

Using questions beginning with *who*, *what*, *when*, *where*, *why* and *how* (WWWWWH) will ensure you gain quality answers. If you would rather use questions with yes/no responses, you could ask a further question to enable your student to elaborate on why they answered yes or no.

Example

Was the assessment activity as you expected? YES/NO

Why was this?

This enables your student to expand on their response, and gives you more information to act on. When designing questionnaires, use the KISS method: *Keep it Short and Simple*. Don't overcomplicate your questions, i.e. by asking two questions in one sentence, or make the questionnaire so long that students will not want to complete it.

You could consider using the Lickert (1932) scale which gives respondents choices to a question such as:

1. strongly disagree

2. disagree

3. neither agree nor disagree

4. agree

5. strongly agree

However, you might find respondents choose option 3 as a safe answer. Removing a middle response and giving four options forces a choice:

1. strongly disagree

2. disagree

3. agree

4. strongly agree

Anonymity should be given for any survey or questionnaire used. If your student is with you at the time, this will not be the case; nor will there be anonymity with telephone or face-to-face questioning. Electronic questionnaires that are e-mailed back will denote who the student is; however, postal ones will not. There are lots of online programs now for surveys that will guarantee anonymity and will also analyse the results of quantitative data.

Searching the internet will give you lots of ideas regarding questionnaire design or programs that could be used to create an online survey.

Always set a date for the return of any surveys and don't be disappointed if you don't get as many replies as you had hoped. Denscombe (2001) predicted a 30 per cent response rate. However, if you give students time to complete a questionnaire perhaps immediately after a session, they will hand it in straight away rather than take it away and forget about it.

Always inform your students why you are asking them to complete the questionnaire and what the information will be used for. Make sure you analyse the results, create an action plan and follow this through, otherwise the process is meaningless. Informing your students of the results and subsequent action keeps them up to date with developments, and shows that you take their feedback seriously.

Another way of obtaining feedback is through *focus groups* – a face-to-face group meeting and discussion. This could be carried out via teleconferencing if everyone cannot attend a certain venue at the same time.

> *Focus groups show signs of taking over from questionnaires ... they share with postal questionnaires the advantages of being an efficient way of generating substantial amounts of data. However, as with questionnaires, these perceived advantages are offset by considerable disadvantages. For example, it is difficult or impossible to follow up the views of individuals, and group dynamics or power hierarchies affect who speaks and what they say.*

(Robson, 2002: 284)

Reflecting upon your own teaching and taking account of feedback from your students and colleagues will enable you to become an effective and professional teacher. Ensuring you embrace equality and diversity within the teaching and learning process will help motivate and encourage your students, promoting a climate of tolerance, trust, respect and achievement.

Extension Activity

Design a short questionnaire that could be used with your students to gain feedback regarding equality and diversity. Consider the types of questions you will ask and how you will ask them, based upon the information you need to ascertain. Decide how the questionnaire will be implemented, i.e. paper based, online, in person, etc. If possible use it with your students by a set date, analyse the results and recommend improvements to be made based on these.

Summary

In this chapter you have learnt about:

- interacting with others;

- sources of information, and external agencies;

- evaluating own practice.

Cross-referencing grid

This chapter contributes towards the following: scope (S), knowledge (K) and practice (P) aspects of the Professional Teaching Standards (A–F domains) and the Equality and Diversity assessment criteria at levels 3 and 4. Full details of the learning outcomes and assessment criteria for the units can be found in the appendices.

Domain	Standards
A	AS2, AS3, AS4, AS5, AS7, AK2.1, AK2.2, AK3.1, AK4.2, AK4.3, AK5.1, AK5.2, AK7.3, AP3.1, AP4.2, AP4.3, AP5.1, AP5.2, AP7.3
B	BS2, BS4, BK1.2, BK2.6, BK2.7, BK3.1, BK3.2, BK3.4, BP2.7, BP3.4, BP3.5, BP4.1, BP5.2
C	CS1, CS2, CS3, CS4, CK4.2, CP3.2, CP3.4, CP4.1
D	DS1, DS3, DK1.1, DK2.1, DK3.1, DK3.2, DP2.1, DP3.2
E	ES4, EK2.1
F	FS1, FS2, FS3, FS4, FK1.1, FK1.2, FK2.1, FK4.2, FP1.2, FP2.1, FP4.1, FP4.2
Equality and Diversity unit	**Assessment criteria**
Level 3	1.2, 2.1, 2.2, 3.1, 3.2, 3.3, 3.4, 4.1, 4.2, 5.1, 5.2
Level 4	1.2, 2.1, 2.2, 3.1, 3.2, 3.3, 3.4, 4.1, 4.2, 5.1, 5.2

Theory focus

References and further information

Allport, GW (1954) *The nature of prejudice*. Reading, MA: Addison-Wesley

Clements, P and Jones, J (2005) *The Diversity Training Handbook: A Practical Guide to Understanding and Changing Attitudes*. London: Kogan Page

Clements, P and Spinks, T (2005) *The Equal Opportunities Handbook*. London: Kogan Page

Denscombe, M (2001) *The Good Research Guide*. Buckingham: Open University Press

Gravells, A and Simpson, S (2008) *Planning and Enabling Learning*. Exeter: Learning Matters

Likert, R (1932) A Technique for the Measurement of Attitudes. *Archives of Psychology*, 140: 1–55

Robson, C (2002) *Real World Research* (2nd edn). Oxford: Blackwell Publishers Ltd

Rose, C (2010) *Brief Guide: Equality Act 2010*. Coventry: Learning and Skills Improvement Service (LSIS)

Schön, D (1983) *The Reflective Practitioner*. London: Temple Smith

Websites

Advice, Conciliation and Arbitration Service (ACAS) – www.acas.org.uk

Equality and Diversity Forum – www.edf.org.uk

Institute for learning – www.ifl.ac.uk

Learner Voice – www.excellencegateway.org.uk/node/2860

Ofsted – www.ofsted.gov.uk

Surveys & questionnaires (free program) – www.surveymonkey.com

6 RELEVANT LEGISLATION

Introduction

In this chapter you will learn about the:

- Apprenticeships, Skills, Children and Learning Act (2009)

- Children Act (2004)

- Data Protection Act (2003)

- Equality Act (2010)

- Freedom of Information Act (2000)

- Human Rights Act (1998)

- Protection from Harassment Act (1997)

- Rehabilitation of Offenders Act (1974)

- Safeguarding Vulnerable Groups Act (2006)

- Work and Families Act (2006)

There are activities and examples to help you reflect on the above which will assist your understanding of the legislation and regulations surrounding equality and diversity in the learning environment.

A cross-referencing grid shows how the content of this chapter contributes towards the Professional Teaching Standards and the Equality and Diversity assessment criteria at Levels 3 and 4. There is also a theory focus with relevant references, further information and websites you might like to refer to.

A vast amount of legislation is currently available which relates to equality and diversity, so not all could be covered comprehensively within this book. This chapter therefore gives a brief overview of that which is most relevant. The information does not constitute legal advice and any errors or omissions are unintentional.

Depending upon whether you work in England, Scotland, Wales or Northern Ireland, there may be some differences with what is stated here; you are therefore advised to check the current legislation for the country in which you work. Most legislation is subject to change; therefore you are also advised to check for any relevant updates or amendments which may have taken place since this book was written.

A search via the internet will soon help you locate further details of each Act and other relevant websites are listed at the end of the chapter.

Apprenticeships, Skills, Children and Learning Act (2009)

This Act introduced a wide range of measures which included:

- the right for employees to request time away from their duties to undertake training; it places a corresponding duty on employers to consider such requests seriously and to be able to refuse them only for specified business reasons;

- provision for a statutory framework for apprenticeships and a right to an apprenticeship for suitably qualified 16–18 year olds.

For the first time, employees were given the legal right to request time to train from their employers, and apprenticeships will receive a boost under new legislation to unlock the potential of individuals and businesses.

By introducing a new right to ask for time for training, employees will be able to talk to employers about their training needs, and employers will become more aware of the public funds available to support training.

Employers will be legally obliged to seriously consider requests for training they receive, but could refuse a request where there was a good business reason to do so. Employers will not be obliged to meet the salary or training costs to enable an employee to take time off to train, but many may choose to do so, recognising the opportunity to invest in their business.

Further information can be found at www.legislation.gov.uk/ukpga/2009/22/contents.

Children Act (2004)

The Children Act (2004) provides the legal underpinning for the *Every Child Matters: Change for Children programme*. *Well-being* is the term used in the Act to define how to help children and young adults achieve more. There are five outcomes:

- be healthy
- stay safe
- enjoy and achieve
- make a positive contribution
- achieve economic well-being

Local authorities and their relevant partners are encouraged to co-operate to improve children's well-being. They need to help all children and young people achieve more and support those who work every day with children, young people and their families to deliver better outcomes. This should lead to children and young people experiencing more integrated and responsive services with specialist support. Staff will work in multi-disciplinary teams, be trained jointly to tackle cultural and professional divides, and be co-located in communities and neighbourhoods.

Strong local partnerships are crucial to meeting the needs of all children and that is why the government intends to remove much of the bureaucracy surrounding children's trusts and allow schools to choose how best they may engage. The current Secretary of State, Michael Gove, has indicated that he intends to:

- remove the duty on schools to co-operate through Children's Trusts via the Education Act (2011)
- remove the requirement on local authorities to set up Children's Trust Boards and the requirement on those Boards to prepare and publish a joint Children and Young People's Plan
- revoke the regulations underpinning the Children and Young People's Plan and withdraw the statutory guidance on children's trusts.

The establishment of a LSCB is an important element of improved child protection.

In June 2010, the Secretary of State for Education commissioned Professor Eileen Munro of the London School of Economics to conduct a wide-ranging independent review to improve child protection. In May 2011, Professor Munro published her final report entitled A *child-centred system*.

Professor Munro's report makes 15 recommendations and signals a shift from previous reforms that, while well-intentioned, resulted in a tick-box culture and a loss of focus on the needs of the child. Taken together, the recommendations cover the following key areas:

- radical reduction in the amount of central prescription to help professionals move from a compliance culture to a learning culture, where they have more freedom to assess need and provide the right help. Statutory guidance should be revised and the inspection process modified to give a clearer focus on children's needs and inspection should be unannounced;

- local authorities and their statutory partners should be given a new duty to secure sufficient provision of early help services for children, young people and families, leading to better identification of the help that is needed and resulting in an offer of early help;

- affirmation of the importance of clear lines of accountability as set out in the Children Act (2004) and the protection of the roles of Director of Children's Services and Lead Members from additional functions, unless there are exceptional circumstances;

- strengthened monitoring of the effectiveness of help and protection by LSCBs, including multi-agency training for safeguarding and child protection.

Activity

Find out if you are likely to be affected by the contents of the Children Act 2004. It could be that you teach students who are under 16 years of age, or vulnerable young people and adults.

Further information can be found at the shortcut http://tinyurl.com/6wu6cax.

Data Protection Act (2003)

This Act is mandatory for all organisations that hold or process personal data. The 1998 Act was extended in 2003 to make reference to electronic data. The Act contains eight principles to ensure that data are:

1. processed fairly and lawfully
2. obtained and used only for specified and lawful purposes
3. adequate, relevant and not excessive
4. accurate and, where necessary, kept up to date

5. kept for no longer than necessary

6. processed in accordance with the individual's rights

7. kept secure

8. transferred only to countries that offer adequate protection

All external stakeholders such as awarding organisations and funding bodies should be aware of your systems of record-keeping as they may need to approve certain records or storage methods.

Confidentiality should be maintained regarding all information you keep.

Further information can be found at http://regulatorylaw.co.uk/Data_Protection.html.

Equality Act (2010)

The Equality Act (2010) replaced the existing anti-discrimination laws with a single Act. It has three main aims:

● to simplify, streamline and harmonise discrimination law

● to strengthen the law

● to support progress in promoting equality and consistently achieving improved outcomes

The Act brings together and re-states all of the following legislation and provision to give a single approach where appropriate, and as a result, most existing legislation will be or has been repealed:

● Civil Partnership Act (2004)

● Disability Discrimination Act (1995)

● Employment Equality (Age) Regulations (2006)

● Employment Equality (Religion or Belief) Regulations (2003)

● Employment Equality (Sexual Orientation) Regulations (2003)

● Equal Pay Act (1970)

● Equality Act (2006), Part 2

● Equality Act (Sexual Orientation) Regulations (2007)

● European Union Employment Directive (2000)

● Race Relations Act (1976)

● Sex Discrimination Act (1975)

The Equality Act (2006) will remain in force (as amended by the 2010 Act) so far as it relates to the constitution and operation of the Equality and Human Rights Commission. The Commission for Equality and Human Rights is responsible for promoting understanding of equality and human rights issues and for challenging unlawful discrimination. It is also responsible for promoting other specific areas of discrimination, for example, sexual orientation, religion or belief, and age, and has a wider general remit to promote human rights and equality generally, even those areas not covered by specific pieces of legislation.

The Equality and Human Rights Commission champions equality and human rights for all, working to eliminate discrimination, reduce inequality, protect human rights and to build good relations, ensuring that everyone has a fair chance to participate in society.

(www.equalityhumanrights.com/wales/
the-commission-in-wales/ (16.11.11))

The Act, which came into force on 6 April 2011, simplifies the law, removes inconsistencies and makes it easier for people to understand and comply with it. It also strengthens the law in important ways to help tackle discrimination and inequality. The Act:

- places a new duty on certain public bodies to consider socio-economic disadvantage when making strategic decisions about how to exercise their functions;

- extends the circumstances in which a person is protected against discrimination, harassment or victimisation because of a protected characteristic;

- extends the circumstances in which a person is protected against discrimination by allowing people to make a claim if they are directly discriminated against because of a combination of two relevant protected characteristics. Combined discrimination (initially referred to as multiple or dual discrimination) is where a person suffers unfavourable treatment because of a combination of two protected characteristics, for example race and sex. The decision to introduce the combined discrimination provision was thought necessary as the law did not provide protection for people who experience a particular disadvantage because of a combination of protected characteristics. A person who experiences such combined discrimination had to bring two separate claims in respect of each protected characteristic, for example race and sex, whereas in fact the real reason for the unfavourable treatment was due to a combination of the person's race and sex.

Example

An older woman applies for a place on a programme as a driving instructor. She is unsuccessful in her application and when she asks for feedback she is told that she was not offered a place because it is not considered suitable training for an older woman. The driving school advises her that they don't think she would have the strength and agility needed to grab the steering wheel or be able to brake quickly. She is told that she would have been appointed had she been an older man or a younger woman because they would be stronger and more able to deal with awkward and difficult customers.

- creates a duty on listed public bodies when carrying out their functions and other persons when carrying out public functions take into consideration the need to:

  - eliminate conduct which the Act prohibits

  - advance equality of opportunity between persons who share a relevant protected characteristic and those who do not

  - foster good relations between people who share a relevant protected characteristic and people who do not

The practical effect is that listed public bodies will have to consider how their policies, programmes and service delivery will affect people with the protected characteristics.

The Act also:

- allows an employer or service provider or other organisation to take positive action so as to enable existing or potential employees or customers to overcome or minimise a disadvantage arising from a protected characteristic

- enables an employment tribunal to make a recommendation to a respondent who has lost a discrimination claim to take certain steps to remedy matters not just for the benefit of the individual claimant (who may have already left the organisation concerned) but also the wider workforce

- amends the Civil Partnership Act (2004) to remove the prohibition on civil partnerships being registered in religious premises

Activity

Find out if your organisation is actively promoting The Equality Act 2010. Is any information displayed on notice boards? Have you been invited to attend any training sessions? Make sure you are aware of the implications of the protected characteristics, and that your colleagues are too.

The Act contains nine protected characteristics which are briefly explained here, along with other aspects such as, Sex, Pay, and Special Educational Needs and Disability:

- age
- disability
- gender
- gender identity
- marriage and civil partnership
- pregnancy and maternity
- race
- religion and belief
- sexual orientation

Further information regarding the Act can be found at the government's Equalities website via the internet shortcut http://tinyurl.com/4uaqoq.

Equality Act (2010): Age

Fairness at work and good job performance go hand in hand. Tackling discrimination helps to attract, motivate and retain staff and enhances the reputation of the employer and the organisation. Eliminating discrimination helps everyone to have an equal opportunity to work and to develop their skills. It is unlawful because of age to:

- directly or indirectly discriminate against anyone
- subject someone to harassment related to age
- victimise someone because of their age

- discriminate against someone, in certain circumstances, after the working relationship has ended, unless objectively justified

- retire an employee compulsorily, unless the retirement can be justified objectively

The law applies to employment and vocational training and prohibits unjustified direct and indirect age discrimination, and all harassment and victimisation on grounds of age, for example retirement.

The Act:

- removes the upper age limit for unfair dismissal and redundancy rights, giving older workers the same rights to claim unfair dismissal or receive a redundancy payment as younger workers, unless there is a genuine retirement

- allows pay and non-pay benefits to continue which depend on length of service requirements of five years or less, or which recognise and reward loyalty and experience and motivate staff

- removes the age limits for Statutory Sick Pay, Statutory Maternity Pay, Statutory Adoption Pay and Statutory Paternity Pay, so that the legislation for all four statutory payments applies in exactly the same way to all

- removes the lower and upper age limits in the Statutory Redundancy Scheme, but leaves the current age banded system in place

- provides exemptions for many age-based rules in occupational pension schemes

A compulsory retirement age is a form of direct age discrimination. However, the Act continues the approach taken in current legislation, by allowing an extension in relation to compulsory retirement age in *schedule 9, paragraph 9*. The government has set a default retirement age of 65, which is allowed under article 6(1) of the Council Directive 2000/78/EC as being justified by reference to a legitimate aim of social policy. Benefits based on length of service, *schedule 9, paragraph 10*, are designed to ensure that employers do not have to justify differences in pay and benefits that have arisen from service of up to five years. An employer can make awards on the basis of five years or more service, if it reasonably believes this fulfils a business need, for example by encouraging loyalty or motivation, or rewarding the experience of staff.

Activity

Look at the resources you are currently using or plan to use with your students. Do they differentiate for students of all ages? Are they inclusive, i.e. are there references to different age groups in any handouts? Are you reliant on using new technology, which older students might not be familiar with? Always make sure your resources and activities are inclusive, and cover the protected characteristics of equality: age; disability; gender, gender reassignment; marriage and civil partnership; pregnancy and maternity; race; religion or belief and sexual orientation.

Further information can be found at the ACAS website: www.acas.org.uk/index.aspx?articleid=1841.

Equality Act (2010): Disability

The Equality Act (2010) protects anyone who has or has had a disability and protects people from:

- being discriminated against and harassed because of a disability they do not personally have;

- being mistakenly perceived to have a disability;

- being discriminated against and harassed because they are associated or linked with people who have a disability;

- having to show that their impairment affects a particular *capacity*, i.e. mobility, speech, hearing or eyesight.

For an impairment to be a disability, its effect on normal day-to-day activities must be *substantial*. Section 212(1) of the Equality Act (2010) now defines substantial to mean *more than minor or trivial*. *Impairment* covers, for example, long-term medical conditions such as asthma and diabetes, and fluctuating or progressive conditions such as rheumatoid arthritis or motor neurone disease. A mental impairment includes mental health conditions (such as bipolar disorder or depression), learning difficulties (such as dyslexia) and learning disabilities (such as autism and Down's syndrome). Some people, including those with cancer, multiple sclerosis and HIV/AIDS, are automatically protected as disabled people by the Act. People with severe disfigurement will be protected as disabled without needing to show that it has a substantial adverse effect on day-to-day activities.

Previously, direct disability discrimination was only unlawful when it happened in relation to work. The Equality Act (2010) means the ban on direct discrimination will now apply in other areas, such as access to goods and services. Direct discrimination occurs where, because of disability, a person receives worse treatment than someone who does not have a disability. This provision is intended to stop people being denied a service, or receiving a worse service, because of prejudice. It is against the law for employers to discriminate against a disabled person because of their disability:

- by deciding who is offered the job, for example, in the way the applications are handled, the way the interview is carried out or through tests used

- in the terms on which they offer a job, for example by just giving a short-term contract

- by asking about sickness absence on application forms

- by asking applicants to complete health and disability-related questionnaires before offering a job; employers can still ask people to complete occupational health questionnaires, providing they are completed after a job has been offered to a candidate

- by refusing or omitting to offer a job

The governing bodies of further education colleges and LEAs providing learning are named as responsible bodies which have an Equality Duty under the legislation. The aim of the Equality Duty is to embed equality considerations into their day-to-day work, so that they tackle discrimination and inequality. The Equality Duty consists of a *general* duty and a *specific* duty:

- *general duty*
  - eliminate unlawful discrimination, harassment and victimisation and other conduct prohibited by the Equality Act (2010)
  - advance equality of opportunity between people of different groups
  - foster good relations between people from different groups
- *specific duty*
  - publication of information showing that they have complied with the general duty
  - evidence of undertaking equality analysis
  - publishing equality objectives
  - publish information about engagement and activities undertaken

The Equality Duty covers all the nine protected characteristics and is designed to help public bodies deliver equality outcomes.

Example

An Adult and Community Learning Service identifies that a large percentage of its students are not disclosing that they have a disability in the early stages of their learning programme. The Service has set an equality objective to encourage students who do have a disability to declare this so that an appropriate level of support can be arranged. The Service has decided how it will measure progress towards the achievement of this objective.

Organisations need to anticipate the likely needs of disabled students and not merely respond to individual needs as they arise. The Act uses a wide definition of disabled person to include: *people with physical or sensory impairments, dyslexia, medical conditions, mental health difficulties and learning difficulties.* Educational organisations have a duty to take reasonable steps to encourage students to disclose a disability. This could be part of the application or interview stage when a student commences with your organisation. This encouragement should be ongoing throughout the programme, in case something occurs which may affect a student's progress.

The Act gives disabled people rights in the areas of:

- employment

- education

- access to goods, facilities and services

- buying or renting land or property, including making it easier for disabled people to rent property and for tenants to make disability-related adaptations

If a student does disclose a disability or additional need to one person, including you as their teacher, then the whole organisation is *deemed to know*. It is therefore important that any issues are communicated to all concerned, and acted upon.

The Equality Act (2010) requires that service providers must think ahead and take steps to address barriers that impede disabled people. In doing this, it is a good idea to consider the range of disabilities that your actual or potential service users might have. You should not wait until a disabled person experiences difficulties using a service, as this may mean it is too late to make the necessary adjustment. Organisations have to make *reasonable adjustments* to the physical features of their premises to overcome physical barriers to access. When deciding what is *reasonable*, how much a change will cost and how much the change would help a student will be taken into consideration. Previously, adjustments to premises and to policies, practices and procedures had to be made by organisations only where it would otherwise be *impossible or unreasonably difficult* for a disabled person to use the service. Now, under the Equality Act, adjustments must be made where disabled people experience a *substantial disadvantage*. This means that organisations may have to make more adjustments and ensure that the adjustment is a reasonable one to make.

Example

Fatima has a student, Marie, who uses a wheelchair. Prior to Marie commencing the programme, Fatima checked all the rooms and facilities that Marie would use, to ensure they were accessible. A special desk was ordered which has adjustable legs that can be raised, and a ramp was installed outside one of the rooms. Signage was also made clearer regarding accessible toilet facilities. As Marie would also need access to the library and computer facilities on the second floor, Fatima checked the lift had controls at a suitable height. She also spoke to the support staff to ensure Fatima could access books and computing equipment.

You can also help your students by organising your environment to enable ease of access around any obstacles (including other students' belongings), along corridors, and around internal and external doors. When teaching, ensure you face your students when speaking to assist anyone hard of hearing, produce clearly printed handouts in a font, size and colour to suit any particular student requirements or use Braille if required. You may have to arrange additional support for some students, to ensure they are not excluded from any activities, and you may need further training yourself to familiarise yourself with particular student requirements.

Always ask your students if there is anything you can do to help make their learning experience a positive one.

Activity

Find out who is responsible within your organisation for arranging or adapting equipment and resources. Talk to them to find out what you would need to do to make a request. It could be that this must be done formally, therefore you would need to allow enough time for actions to take place. You might need to borrow equipment from other departments and there may be a booking system for this.

Further information can be found at the Directgov website: www.direct.gov.uk/en/DisabledPeople/index.htm.

Equality Act (2010): Gender and Gender Identity

The Act makes it illegal to discriminate on the grounds of gender reassignment, however only in the areas of employment and vocational training. They do not cover the provision of goods, facilities or services. Gender reassignment is defined as a process, which is undertaken under medical supervision for the purposes of reassigning a person's sex by changing physiological or other characteristics of sex, and includes any part of such a process.

The definition of gender reassignment has been amended so that people no longer have to be under medical supervision to be protected by the law. Section 7 of the Act defines the protected characteristic of gender reassignment as *where a person has proposed, started or completed a process to change his or her sex*. A transsexual person has the protected characteristic of gender reassignment.

In addition to direct and indirect discrimination, protection remains for people undergoing gender reassignment from discrimination due to absence from work. Where a transsexual person is absent from work because of gender reassignment, the Act provides that they should be treated no less favourably than if the absence was due to sickness or injury or another reason, for example caring for a relative.

The Act enables people who meet the requirements to change their legal gender. This includes the right to a new birth certificate, if the birth was registered in the UK, and provides recognition of a person's acquired gender for all legal purposes. This means that the person must be regarded as their acquired gender in all aspects of life. Under the Act, people who are at least 18 years of age are eligible to formally apply for a Gender

Recognition Certificate (GRC) if they have:

- officially changed their name (if necessary);
- been living full-time in their acquired gender for over two years, and intend to do so permanently;
- been diagnosed as having gender dysphoria.

Surgery or any other gender reassignment treatment, such as hormone therapy, is not a prerequisite to obtaining a certificate. Once a person has their GRC, they must be regarded as a member of their acquired gender for all purposes, including legal records. This means that a female-to-male trans man with a GRC can apply for a job where being male is a *genuine occupational qualification*, for example as a male care assistant. Knowledge about a person's gender recognition is regarded as *protected information*. Anyone who acquires such knowledge in the course of their official duties and then passes it on to a third party without the trans person's consent may be prosecuted and fined.

In April 2007, the *Forum on Sexual Orientation and Gender Identity in Post-School Education* was established, bringing together relevant bodies in further and higher education. Its aim is to co-ordinate work on sexual orientation and gender identity equality, and to share expertise. A document called *Guidance on trans equality in post school education* has been produced which provides background information, practical advice and examples of best practice to help post-16 educational establishments take positive steps to fulfil their legal requirements, and provide a positive environment for trans workers and students.

Activity

Access the website via the internet shortcut http://tinyurl.com/d257az9, and have a look at the variety of guidance available on trans equality. Reading the contents will increase your knowledge and understanding.

Further information can be found at the Press for Change website: http://transequality.co.uk/default.aspx.

Equality Act (2010): Marriage and Civil Partnership

The Equality Act (2010) defines the protected characteristic of marriage and civil partnership as people who have or share the common characteristics of being married or of being a civil partner. *Marriage* is defined as a *union between a man and a woman*. Same-sex couples can have their relationships legally recognised as *civil partnerships*. Civil partners must be treated the same as married couples on a wide range of legal matters. It is prohibited for civil partnerships to include religious readings, music or symbols and for the ceremonies to take place in religious venues. On 17 February 2011, the UK government announced that, as a result of the passing of the Equality Act (2010), it would bring forward the necessary measures to remove these restrictions in England and Wales, although religious venues would not be compelled to offer civil partnerships.

Further information can be found at the Directgov website via the internet shortcut http://tinyurl.com/7rlvwcu.

Equality Act (2010): Maternity and Pregnancy

It is unlawful for an employer to dismiss someone because they are pregnant or for reasons connected with pregnancy or maternity leave. It is also unlawful for an employer to deny access to holiday pay, sickness pay, training or any other contractual benefit that all employees are entitled to.

Pregnancy is not an illness, therefore females do not suddenly become less capable of doing their job as a result.

The Act covers aspects such as entitlement to ordinary and additional maternity leave, sick pay during pregnancy-related illness and when to return after having a baby.

Further information can be found at the Equality and Human Rights Commission website via the internet shortcut http://tinyurl.com/73frtfw.

Equality Act (2010): Race

The Act makes it illegal to discriminate on the grounds of:

- colour
- ethnic or national origin
- nationality (including citizenship)
- race

It applies to discrimination in employment and vocational training, education, housing and the provision of goods, facilities and services.

This includes:

- benefits granted by employers

- choosing successful applicants

- dismissal, disciplinary hearings

- opportunities for promotion

- terms of employment

- the selection process

- transfers or training

- unfair treatment of employees

Example

Paul was due to take an evening class of 20 adult students wanting to achieve Advanced Level Mathematics. He noticed two names on the list which sounded Polish. Paul telephoned them prior to the start date, and persuaded them not to attend. He advised them to take a GCSE instead. Paul was concerned that they would not achieve, therefore affecting his retention and achievement rates. In reality, it turned out the prospective students were English and had Polish surnames by marriage. Paul had made a wrong assumption and broken the law by discriminating.

Further information can be found at the Commission for Equality and Human Rights website via the internet shortcut http://tinyurl.com/7uhhttv.

Equality Act (2010): Religion and Belief

The Equality Act (2010) protects people from discriminatory practices based on actual or perceived religion, or similar belief defined as *religion, religious belief or similar philosophical belief*. Harassment is unlawful whether it is on the grounds of your actual or supposed religious belief or even on the grounds of the religious belief of the people you associate with. Harassment of someone because they are perceived to be Muslim will be unlawful whether they are Muslim or not.

The Act makes the following illegal:

- direct discrimination – treating people less favourably than others on the grounds of their religion or belief

- indirect discrimination – applying a provision, criterion or practice which disadvantages people of a particular religion or belief which is not justified as a proportionate means of achieving a legitimate aim

- harassment – unwanted conduct that violates people's dignity or creates an intimidating, hostile, degrading, humiliating or offensive environment

- victimisation – treating people less favourably because of something they have done under or in connection with the Act, for example made a formal complaint of discrimination or given evidence in a tribunal case

The legislation therefore means schools and colleges:

- cannot refuse access to training, or to promotion, on the basis of religion or belief

- must act to protect employees against bullying or harassment suffered on the grounds of religion or belief; the perception of the person suffering the harassment is crucial

- cannot deny workers benefits, facilities and services that they offer to other employees, for example insurance schemes, travel concessions or social events, on the basis of religion or belief

- cannot give an unfair reference when someone leaves because of their religion or belief

Example

Jack was reviewing applications from prospective students for a one week's Exercise to Music programme. The maximum number he could take was 12, but he had 16 applicants. Four of these were Muslim; Jack therefore decided he would not accept them as he did not want to offend them. He was concerned they would complain about the dress code, and that they would not attend at various times because they would want to pray.

In this example, Jack was directly discriminating against the four Muslim applicants and therefore breaking the law.

Further information can be found at the National Union of Teachers website: www.teachers.org.uk/taxonomy/term/271.

Equality Act: Sexual Orientation

Under the Equality Act (2010) it is unlawful to discriminate against someone due to their sexual orientation. The Act protects people from discriminatory practices based on actual or perceived sexual orientation defined as *heterosexual, gay, lesbian or bisexual*. Harassment is unlawful whether it is on the grounds of your actual or supposed sexual orientation or even on the grounds of the sexual orientation of the people you associate with. Harassment of someone because he is perceived to be gay will be unlawful whether he is gay or not.

The Act makes the following illegal:

- direct discrimination – treating people less favourably than others on the grounds of their actual or perceived sexual orientation

- indirect discrimination – applying a provision, criterion or practice which disadvantages people of a particular sexual orientation, unless it can be objectively justified

- harassment – unwanted conduct that violates people's dignity or creates an intimidating, hostile, degrading, humiliating or offensive environment

- victimisation – treating people less favourably because they have made or intend to make a complaint or allegation in relation to a complaint of discrimination on the grounds of sexual orientation

Example

Fiona complained to her teacher that she was being harassed by a couple of other students in the group. She had recently informed her peers she was a lesbian and felt this was the reason why. Rather than embarrass Fiona or draw attention to the students in question, her teacher amended her next session plan to include a discussion about equality and diversity. The harassment stopped once the students had gained a better understanding of how to embrace people's differences.

Further information can be found at the ACAS website: www.acas.org.uk/index.aspx?articleid=1824.

Equality Act (2010): Sex

The Act makes it illegal to discriminate on the grounds of sex in:

- employment and vocational training
- education
- housing
- the provision of goods, facilities and services

The Act is intended to put into effect *the principle of equal treatment for men and women as regards access to employment, including promotion, and to vocational training*. Changes to the Act mean that employers could be liable for sexual harassment of employees by third parties, for example customers, parents, contractors, providing the employer is aware that this has happened earlier on more than two occasions and has failed to take reasonable steps to stop it. The Act extends third party harassment to cover all protected characteristics except pregnancy and maternity, and marriage and civil partnerships.

Further information can be found at the government's Equalities website via the internet shortcut http://tinyurl.com/3fhjjf.

Equality Act (2010): Pay

The equal pay provisions in the Act came into force on 1 October 2010 to eliminate discrimination between men and women in terms of their pay and contracts of employment. This relates to:

- work that is the same or broadly similar
- work rated as equivalent under a job evaluation study
- work of equal value in terms of the demands made on them under headings such as effort, skill and decision-making

The Act gives men and women the right to equality in the terms of their contract of employment. It covers pay and other terms and conditions such as piecework, output and bonus payments, holidays and sick leave.

European law has extended the concept of equal pay to include redundancy payments, travel concessions, employers' pension contributions and occupational pension benefits. This means that even though a man and a woman are receiving the same basic rate of pay, there may still be a breach of the principle of equal pay because other benefits (such as a company car, private health care, etc.) are not provided on an equal basis.

The Act relates to pay or benefits provided by a contract of employment, and applies to all employers irrespective of their size, and whether they are in the public or private sector.

Further information can be found at the government's Equalities website via the internet shortcut http://tinyurl.com/5ytphb.

Equality Act (2010): Special Educational Needs and Disability

The Act has simplified and strengthened discrimination laws to protect those most vulnerable from unfair treatment. The Department for Education has produced a range of guidance to support those students with Special Educational Needs which you can access at: www.education.gov.uk/schools/pupilsupport/sen/guidance.

It is unlawful for a college or further education provider to treat a disabled student unfavourably. Such treatment could amount to:

- direct discrimination – an education provider must not treat a disabled student less favourably simply because of their disability, for instance they can't refuse admission to disabled applicants because they are disabled

- indirect discrimination – an education provider must not do something for all students which would have a negative effect on disabled students, unless they have a genuine reason, for example only providing course application forms in one format, which may not be accessible to disabled people

- discrimination arising from a disability – an education provider must not discriminate against a student because of something that is a consequence of their disability, for example they can't stop a disabled student going outside at break time because it takes them too long to get there

- harassment – an education provider must not harass a student because of their disability, for example a teacher must not shout at a disabled student, if due to their disability, they are unable to concentrate

If a disabled person is at a substantial disadvantage, responsible bodies are required to take reasonable steps to prevent that disadvantage. This could include:

- changes to policies and practices

- changes to programme requirements or work placements

- changes to the physical features of a building

- the provision of an interpreter or other support staff

- the provision of resources in other formats

The reasonable steps taken will depend upon:

- the type of services being provided
- the nature of the institution or service and its size and resources
- the effect of the disability on the individual disabled person or student

If necessary, the final decision about what is reasonable will be decided by the courts.

Activity

Find out what you should do to help a student who discloses to you that they have a disability. Also, check your organisation's application forms to ensure a question is asked to enable a prospective student to inform you of any disability that may affect their learning. Some students may not consider they have a disability, and therefore not disclose it. It is important to encourage your students to discuss anything with you that may affect their attendance or the learning process.

Student services covered by the Act can include a wide range of educational and non-educational services, for example field trips, catering facilities, examinations and assessments, arrangements for work placements, libraries and learning resources.

Further information can be found at the Directgov website via the internet shortcut http://tinyurl.com/3zkrpr.

Freedom of Information Act (2000)

This Act gives people the opportunity to request to see the information public authorities hold about them.

Further information can be found at www.opsi.gov.uk/Acts/acts2000/ukpga_20000036_en_1.

Human Rights Act (1998)

The Human Rights Act (1998) came into force in October 2000. All people should have basic rights which include:

- the right to life (Article 2)

- freedom from torture or inhuman or degrading treatment (Article 3)

- freedom from slavery or forced labour (Article 4)

- personal freedom (Article 5)

- the right to a fair trial (Article 6)

- no punishment without law (Article 7)

- private life and family (Article 8)

- freedom of belief (Article 9)

- free expression (Article 10)

- free assembly and association (Article 11)

- marriage (Article 12)

- freedom from discrimination (Article 14)

Article 14 of the European Convention on Human Rights states that:

> The enjoyment of the rights and freedoms set forth in this Convention shall be secured without discrimination on any grounds such as sex, race, colour, language, religion, political or other opinion, national or social origin, association with a national minority, property, birth or other status.

All public bodies are required to adhere to the Act and the courts must interpret UK law in accordance with the European Convention on Human Rights and Fundamental Freedoms.

To date, Article 11 has not been interpreted by the European Court of Human Rights to entitle employees to time off on religious holidays or days of rest. Article 10 has not been interpreted to give employees the right to wear what they like to work. However, UK law makes discrimination against a person on the basis of their religion or belief illegal.

Article 8 may be of importance where employers interfere with communications by staff, such as intercepting telephone calls, email or interfering with internet use. The disclosure of personal information about an employee to third parties without that employee's consent may breach Article 8, particularly if it is confidential medical information, which is also illegal under Data Protection legislation.

Further information can be found at the Department for Constitutional Affairs website via the internet shortcut http://tinyurl.com/tmqq9.

Protection from Harassment Act (1997)

The Protection from Harassment Act (1997) introduced four new criminal offences:

- harassment: six months' imprisonment and/or a fine;
- fear of violence: five years' imprisonment and/or a fine on indictment;
- breach of civil injunction: five years' imprisonment and/or a fine on indictment;
- breach of restraining order: five years' imprisonment and/or a fine on indictment.

Further information can be found at the Crown Prosecution Service website: www.cps.gov.uk/index.html.

Rehabilitation of Offenders Act (1974)

The Rehabilitation of Offenders Act (1974) came into force in July 1975 (except for Northern Ireland). Anyone who has been convicted of a criminal offence, and received a sentence of not more than two and a half years in prison, will benefit as a result of the Act, providing they are not convicted again during a specified period otherwise known as the *rehabilitation period*. The length of this period depends on the sentence given for the original offence, and runs from the date of the conviction. If the person does not re-offend during this rehabilitation period, they become a *rehabilitated person*, and their conviction becomes *spent* or is ignored.

Sentences can carry fixed or variable rehabilitation periods and these periods can be extended if the person offends again during the rehabilitation period. However, if the sentence is more than two and a half years in prison, the conviction will never be spent. It is the sentence imposed by the courts that counts, even if it is a suspended sentence, not the time actually spent in prison.

Once a conviction is spent, the convicted person does not have to reveal it or admit its existence (in most circumstances). The two main exceptions relate to working with children or working with the elderly or sick people. If a person wants to apply for a position that involves working with children or working with the elderly or sick people, they are required to reveal all convictions, both spent and unspent.

The Criminal Records Bureau (CRB) is an Executive Agency of the Home Office, which provides access to criminal record information through a disclosure service. If you work with children or vulnerable adults, you will need to provide proof or be subject to a CRB check.

Further information can be found at the Criminal Records Bureau website via the internet shortcut http://tinyurl.com/4ccndo.

Safeguarding Vulnerable Groups Act (2006)

The Safeguarding Vulnerable Groups Act (2006) was passed as a result of the Bichard Inquiry arising from the Soham murders in 2002, when two schoolgirls were murdered by a school caretaker. The Inquiry questioned the way employers recruit people to work with vulnerable groups, and particularly the way background checks are carried out. Recommendation 19 of the Inquiry Report highlighted the need for a single agency to vet all individuals who want to work or volunteer with children or vulnerable adults and to bar unsuitable people from doing so.

Safeguarding is a term used to refer to the duties and responsibilities that those providing a health, social or education service have to perform to protect individuals and vulnerable people from harm. Following the publication of the Safeguarding Vulnerable Groups Act in 2006, a vetting and barring scheme was established in autumn 2008. This Act created an Independent Barring Board to take all discretionary decisions on whether individuals should be barred from working with children and/or vulnerable adults. You will be bound by this Act if you work with children (those under the age of 18 years in training) and/or vulnerable adults. You will need to attend Safeguarding training every three years (every two years for some staff depending upon their Safeguarding involvement).

A vulnerable adult is defined as a person aged 18 years or over, who is in receipt of or may be in need of community care services by reason of 'mental or other disability, age or illness and who is or may be unable to take care of him or herself, or unable to protect him or herself against significant harm or exploitation'.

(Bonnerjea, 2009: 9)

This could be anyone needing formal help to live in society, for example a young mother, someone with a learning disability or a recently released prisoner. If your organisation is inspected by Ofsted, they will be asking your students how safe they feel and whether they are able to give you feedback regarding any concerns they may have.

You have a duty of care and a personal responsibility towards all your students and should apply six key elements of appropriate service provision:

- choice
- confidentiality
- dignity
- independence
- individuality
- respect

There are four key processes that should be followed to ensure your students are safe:

1. an assessment of their needs
2. planning services to meet these needs
3. intervention if necessary when you have a concern
4. reviewing the services offered

If you have any concerns regarding a student, for example if you feel they are being bullied or may be at risk of harm or abuse, you must refer to your DSO immediately. It would be useful to find out who this person is if you don't already know. Never be tempted to get personally involved with your student's situation.

Further information can be found at www.isa-gov.org/default.aspx?page=321.

Work and Families Act (2006)

The Work and Families Act (2006) is the first step towards delivery of some of the measures set out in the government's response to the consultation, *Work and Families: Choice and Flexibility*. The legislation aims to support both employers and working families by providing a framework of rights and responsibilities for both employer and employee. This includes:

- adoption leave and pay
- flexible working and work life balance

- maternity leave and pay

- paternity leave and pay

- additional paternity leave and pay

- parental leave

- part-time work

- time off to support dependants

Further information can be found at the Business, Innovation and Skills website via the internet shortcut http://tinyurl.com/7muh8sg.

Summary

In this chapter you have learnt about the:

- Apprenticeships, Skills, Children and Learning Act (2009)

- Children Act (2004)

- Data Protection Act (2003)

- Equality Act (2010)

- Freedom of Information Act (2000)

- Human Rights Act (1998)

- Protection from Harassment Act (1997)

- Rehabilitation of Offenders Act (1974)

- Safeguarding Vulnerable Groups Act (2006)

- Work and Families Act (2006)

Cross-referencing grid

This chapter contributes towards the following: scope (S), knowledge (K) and practice (P) aspects of the Professional Teaching Standards (A–F) domains) and the Equality and Diversity assessment criteria at levels 3 and 4. Full details of the learning outcomes and assessment criteria for the units can be found in the appendices.

Domain	Standards
A	AS1, AS2, AS3, AS4, AS5, AS6, AS7, AK3.1, AK6.1, AK6.2, AP5.1, AP5.2, AP6.1, AP6.2
B	BK4.1, BP3.5, BP4.1
C	
D	DS1
E	
F	FS2, FS4, FK1.1, FK2.1, FK4.1, FK4.2; FP1.1, FP2.1, FP4.1, FP4.2
Equality and Diversity unit	**Assessment criteria**
Level 3	1.3
Level 4	1.3

Theory focus

References and further information

Bonnerjea, L (2009) *Safeguarding Adults Report on the consultation on the review of 'No Secrets'*. London: Department of Health

Department for Education and Skills (DfES) (2006) *Safeguarding Children and Safer Recruitment in Education*. London: DfES

HMI (2008) *Safeguarding Children*. London: Ofsted

Press for Change (2007) *Guidance on trans equality in post school education*. London: Unison

Websites

All Government legislation and regulations can be found at – www.opsi.gov.uk

Business, Innovation and Skills – www.bis.gov.uk

Criminal Records Bureau – www.crb.gov.uk

Department for Education – www.education.gov.uk

Equality Act 2010 – www.legislation.gov.uk/ukpga/2010/15/notes/division/2/1

Equality and Diversity Forum – www.edf.org.uk

Equality and Human Rights Commission – www.equalityhumanrights.com

Equality for Lesbians, Gay Men and Bisexuals – www.stonewall.org.uk

Legal and human rights organisation – www.justice.org.uk

Mental health – www.mind.org.uk

Migrant Workers Gateway – www.migrantgateway.eu

Refugee council – www.refugeecouncil.org.uk

Shortcut website addresses – www.tinyurl.com

Terence Higgins Trust – www.tht.org.uk.

UNIT TITLE: Equality and diversity in the Lifelong Learning Sector LEVEL 3

(6 credits)

Learning Outcomes The learner will:	Assessment Criteria The learner can:	
1 Understand the key features of a culture which promotes equality and values diversity	1.1	Explain the meaning and benefits of diversity and the promotion of equality
	1.2	Explain forms of inequality and discrimination and their impact on individuals, communities and society
	1.3	Identify and outline the relevant legislation, employment regulations and policies and codes of practice relevant to the promotion of equality and valuing of diversity
2 Understand the importance of the promotion of equality and valuing of diversity for effective work in the sector	2.1	Explain how the promotion of equality and diversity can protect people from risk of harm
	2.2	Explain action taken to value individuals and its impact
	2.3	Explain good practice in providing individuals with information
3 Understand and demonstrate behaviour appropriate to the promotion of equality and valuing of diversity	3.1	Explain and demonstrate ways of communication and behaviour which support equality and diversity
	3.2	Explain impact of own behaviour on individuals and their experience of the organisation's culture and approach
	3.3	Explain how own behaviour can impact on own organisation's culture
	3.4	Explain how working with other agencies can promote diversity
4 Understand how to actively help others in the promotion of equality and valuing of diversity	4.1	Describe actions by individuals which can undermine equality and diversity and review strategies for dealing with these effectively
	4.2	Explain strategies for dealing with systems and structures which do not promote equality and diversity
5 Understand how to review own contribution to promoting equality and valuing diversity	5.1	Identify own strengths and areas for development in promoting equality and valuing diversity, using reflection and feedback from individuals
	5.2	Identify and use appropriate sources for support in promoting equality and valuing diversity, explaining why this is necessary

UNIT TITLE: Equality and diversity in the Lifelong Learning Sector LEVEL 4

(6 credits)

Learning Outcomes The learner will:	Assessment Criteria The learner can:	
1 Understand the key features of a culture which promotes equality and values diversity	1.1	Analyse the meaning and benefits of diversity and the promotion of equality
	1.2	Analyse forms of inequality and discrimination and their impact on individuals, communities and society
	1.3	Discuss how relevant legislation, employment regulations and policies and codes of practice contribute to the promotion of equality and valuing of diversity
2 Understand the importance of the promotion of equality and valuing of diversity for effective work in the sector	2.1	Discuss how the promotion of equality and diversity can protect people from risk of harm
	2.2	Evaluate action taken to value individuals and its impact
	2.3	Summarise and demonstrate good practice in providing individuals with information
3 Understand and demonstrate behaviour appropriate to the promotion of equality and valuing of diversity	3.1	Explain and demonstrate ways of communication and behaviour which support equality and diversity
	3.2	Analyse impact of own behaviour on individuals and their experience of the organisation's culture and approach
	3.3	Review the impact of own behaviour on own organisation's culture
	3.4	Explain and demonstrate how working with other agencies can promote diversity
4 Understand how to actively help others in the promotion of equality and valuing of diversity	4.1	Analyse actions by individuals which can undermine equality and diversity and evaluate strategies for dealing with these effectively
	4.2	Evaluate strategies for dealing with systems and structures which do not promote equality and diversity
5 Understand how to review own contribution to promoting equality and valuing diversity	5.1	Evaluate own strengths and areas for development in promoting equality and valuing diversity, using reflection and feedback from individuals
	5.2	Identify, use and evaluate appropriate sources for support in promoting equality and valuing diversity

Abbreviations and Acronyms

ACL – Adult and Community Learning

ACAS – Arbitration and Conciliation Service

ADHD – Attention Deficit Hyperactivity Disorder

ADS – Adult Dyslexia Support

ALN – Adult Literacy and Numeracy

ATLS – Associate Teacher Learning and Skills

BCoDP – British Council of Disabled People

BIHR – British Institute of Human Rights

BIS – Department for Business, Innovation and Skills

BME – Black and Minority Ethnic

CCEA – Council for the Curriculum, Examinations and Assessment (Northern Ireland)

CEHR – Commission for Equality and Human Rights

Cert Ed – Certificate in Education

CPD – Continuing Professional Development

CRB – Criminal Records Bureau

CTLLS – Certificate in Teaching in the Lifelong Learning Sector

DCELLS – Department for Children, Education, Lifelong Learning and Skills (Wales)

DEE – Disability Equality in Education

DSO – Designated Safeguarding Officer

DTLLS – Diploma in Teaching in the Lifelong Learning Sector

EDAR – Experience, Describe, Analyse, Revise

EDF – Equality and Diversity Forum

EHRC – Equality and Human Rights Commission

EQA – External Quality Assurer

ESOL – English for Speakers of Other Languages

GCSE – General Certificate of Secondary Education

GED – Gender Equality Duty

GOQ – Genuine Occupational Qualification

GRC – Gender Recognition Certificate

HEI – Higher Education Institute

HMI – Her Majesty's Inspectorate

HSE – Health and Safety Executive

IAG –Information, Advice and Guidance

ICT – Information Communication Technology

IfL – Institute for Learning

ILT – Information Learning Technology

ILP – Individual Learning Plan

IQA – Internal Quality Assurer

IT – Information Technology

JCP – Job Centre Plus

LADO – Local Authority Designated Officer

LARA – Learning Aim Reference Application

LEA – Local Education Authority

LLN – Language, Literacy, Numeracy

LLUK – Lifelong Learning UK

LSCB – Local Safeguarding Children Board

LSIS – Learning and Skills Improvement Service

NEET – Not in Employment, Education or Training

NIACE – National Institute of Adult Continuing Education

Ofqual – Office of qualifications and examinations regulation

Ofsted – Office for Standards in Education, Children's Services and Skills

PCET – Post Compulsory Education and Training

PGCE – Post Graduate Certificate in Education

PTLLS – Preparing to Teach in the Lifelong Learning Sector

QCF – Qualifications and Credit Framework

QIA – Quality Improvement Agency

QTLS – Qualified Teacher Learning and Skills

RNIB – Royal National Institute for the Blind

RNID – Royal National Institute for the Deaf

SES – Single Equality Scheme

SFA – Skills Funding Agency

SMART – Specific, Measurable, Achievable, Realistic, and Time bound

TAQA – Training, Assessment and Quality Assurance

TUC – Trades Union Congress

VACSR – Valid, Authentic, Current, Sufficient, Reliable

VARK – Visual, Aural, Read/Write, Kinaesthetic

VLE – Virtual Learning Environment

VQ – Vocational Qualification

YPLA – Young People's Learning Agency

Glossary of Terms

Ability – the power or skill needed to do something, usually physical or mental.

Advance – to move forward, to get somewhere, to achieve improved outcomes.

Age – the period of time a person has been living.

Appreciate – to recognise that something is important or valuable.

Association discrimination – discrimination against someone because they associate with a person who has a protected characteristic

Attitude – to speak or act in a way that makes values and beliefs very clear to others.

Barrier – anything that prevents people from accessing something, or understanding others.

Behaviour – actions or reactions to situations or circumstances.

Belief – feeling certain that something is true or exists.

Challenge – to question whether something is true, exists or is legal.

Citizen – an inhabitant of a country, town or city, who may be entitled to some privileges as a result.

Civil ceremony – a non-religious legal partnership between members of the opposite sex.

Civil partnership – a legal partnership between members of the same sex.

Class – a group of people in society who have the same position, for example, social or economic.

Colour – the natural colour of a person's skin by birth.

Culture – the beliefs and customs of a particular group of people.

Dependant – a person who depends on another for support.

Differentiation – the process of recognising something as being different.

Direct discrimination – being treated less favourably than another person in the same situation because they have a protected characteristic.

Disability – a condition, illness or injury that makes it difficult for a person to do the same things others can do.

Discrimination – treating a person or group differently, often in a negative manner.

Diverse – different or varied in some way.

Diversity – valuing the individual differences of a person.

Domestic circumstances – belonging to, or relating to the family house or home.

Dysphoria – an unpleasant or uncomfortable mood, anxiety, irritability, or restlessness, the opposite of euphoria.

Education – the process of teaching or learning.

Employment status – when a person is paid to carry out a relevant job role.

Equal – of the same importance and deserving the same treatment.

Equal opportunity – the principle of treating all people the same.

Equality Act (2010) – legislation aimed at streamlining, harmonising and strengthening the law.

Equality – enjoying equal rights, being of the same importance and receiving the same treatment. A revised term for Equal Opportunities and based on the legal obligation to comply with anti-discrimination legislation.

Ethical – something which is morally right.

Ethnic minority – a national or racial group of people living in a country or area which contains a larger group of people of a different nationality or race.

Ethnic origin – where a national or racial group of people were born.

Ex-offender – person with a criminal record or criminal history.

Exclude – to keep out or omit.

Experience – skills, knowledge and/or attitudes obtained from various activities.

External Quality Assurer – a representative from an external awarding organisation.

Fair – treating others in a way that is reasonable and right.

Faith – a strong belief, often religious.

Fostering – encouraging the development of something.

Gender – the differences between men and women.

Gender reassignment – the modification of a person's biological sex characteristics, by surgery and hormone treatment, to approximate those of the opposite sex.

Grievance – a concern, problem or complaint.

Harassment – behaviour likely to annoy or upset another person.

Human rights – the basic rights which it is generally considered all people should have, for example justice and freedom to speak.

Illegal – prohibited by law or official rules and regulations.

Immigrant – a person who permanently settles in another country after leaving their own.

Inclusive – involving everyone, treating them all equally and fairly, without directly or indirectly excluding anyone.

Indirect discrimination – when there are rules that apply to every-one but affect an individual or group of people more than others, without good reason.

Inequality – a lack of equality or fair treatment between people.

Integration – the process of combining a group of people, for example a minority group, with members of a majority group.

Internal Quality Assurer – an occupationally competent person appointed by the organisation to assure the quality of the work assessed.

Intersectional discrimination – treating a person less favourably on more than one ground simultaneously, the grounds not being separated, for example female and Asian.

Labelling – using word/words to describe someone or something, although usually applied to people.

Language – a system of communication used by people of a particular country or profession.

Learning difficulties – mental problems which affect a person's ability to learn things.

Marital status – whether or not a person is married.

Migrant – a person who moves from one region or area to another.

Minority – a small group of people who are different from the majority.

Modified grievance – a shorter grievance procedure for a person who has left employment.

Moral – behaving in ways considered by most people to be correct and honest.

Multidimensional discrimination – discrimination on more than one ground; the grounds could be separated depending upon the circumstances, for example age and disability.

National origin – where a person's ancestors come from, for example, a particular country, heritage or background.

Nationality – the official right to belong to a particular country or countries.

Offend – to upset a person or make them angry.

Oppose – to disagree with a person or something.

Others – carers, children, colleagues, employers, family, friends, local community, mentors, parents, partners.

Parental status – the status of one person in respect to another, the other being under the age of 18 (or who is 18 or older but is incapable of self-care because of a physical or mental disability). Examples include a biological parent; an adoptive parent; a foster parent; a step-parent; a legal guardian.

Perception discrimination – discrimination against someone because they are perceived to have a protected characteristic.

Policy – a set of ideas that has been agreed officially by a group of people.

Protected characteristic – aspects of a person's identity explicitly protected from discrimination. There are nine identified characteristics: age, disability, gender, gender reassignment, marriage and civil partnerships, pregnancy and maternity, race, religion or belief, sexual orientation.

Political conviction – opinions about how a country should be governed.

Positive discrimination – the practice of giving advantage to those groups in society which are often treated unfairly, usually because of race or sex.

Prejudice – an unfair and unreasonable view or judgement.

Race – a group of people, with similar characteristics.

Racism – the character and behaviour which is influenced by a person's race against another race.

Racist – a person who treats other races unfairly, as they believe they are not as good as their own race.

Reasonable – being fair.

Reasonable adjustments – an employer has a duty to make reasonable adjustments where arrangements or physical premises could place a disabled person at a substantial disadvantage to a person who is not disabled.

Recognise – to accept something, based on experience.

Religion – any system of belief and/or worship.

Respect – to accept or admire.

Reverse discrimination – when an advantage is given to people who are typically thought to be treated unfairly, usually because of their race or sex.

Rights – the claim which a person has to be treated in a fair, morally acceptable or legal way.

Sex – being male or female.

Sexual orientation – relating to being male or female.

Social background – a person's family and experiences, for example education, wealth, living conditions, etc.

Statutory grievance – a three-step procedure all workplaces must have.

Stereotype – a fixed, commonly held notion or image, which is possibly wrong.

Tolerant – to accept the behaviour and beliefs of others, even if not agreeing or approving of them.

Tradition – principles, beliefs or a way of life which people have followed for a long time.

Transgender or transperson – a person whose identity does not conform to conventional ideas of male or female. It ranges from how a person dresses to a person who has multiple surgical operations to reassign to their preferred gender role.

Unethical – something which is morally wrong.

Unfair – unreasonable or not right.

Value – the importance placed upon a person or something.

Victimisation – unfavourable treatment of a person.

Vulnerable – a person who could easily be hurt, for example emotionally, physically or mentally.

Checklist for Advancing Equality and Diversity

Identifying needs

☐ Do your publicity, recruitment and guidance materials contain all the information needed to represent all those for whom it is intended?

☐ Do you provide information, advice and guidance to help students choose the right programme, or progress to a relevant programme?

☐ Is the application and interview process fair to all?

☐ Can you identify any potential learning difficulties and take reasonable steps to address these?

☐ Are your students given the opportunity to discuss why they have chosen your programme, what it is they aspire to, any potential or additional support requirements and needs, and any barriers to learning?

☐ Does your student need to make an appointment to access information, advice and guidance from Next Step? (https://nextstep.direct.gov.uk)

☐ Do you need to make reasonable adjustments to the environment, equipment and/or resources in any way, based on these requirements?

☐ Do your students have the opportunity to take a learning styles test?

☐ Can students take an initial assessment relating to language, literacy, numeracy and ICT if relevant?

☐ Is there a specific initial assessment/skill scan/diagnostic test available in your subject area to help identify a student's current skills and knowledge?

☐ Is there an opportunity for your students to take a dyslexia test?

☐ Can you agree a differentiated individual learning plan with each of your students?

Planning learning

☐ Does your scheme of work reflect the subject in a diverse, yet inclusive way?

☐ Does your scheme of work reflect the requirements of the Ofsted common inspection framework (if applicable), embrace equality and diversity and reflect differentiation?

☐ Does your scheme of work build upon topics in a logical way, taking into account any identified needs, the results of learning styles tests and initial assessment results?

☐ Does your scheme of work take into account any specialist dates that students may not be able to attend, or dates that can be celebrated?

☐ Can you provide a choice of learning opportunities at a variety of times and places?

☐ Can you plan time for tutorials – group and individual? Group tutorials can be an opportunity for equality and diversity activities and discussions to raise awareness.

☐ Does the teaching environment you have been allocated fulfil the needs of your subject and students? Is it safe and accessible?

☐ Do your session plans take into consideration the individual needs of your students, for example level of achievement, learning styles, disabilities, religion, faith, etc.?

☐ Do you use an induction checklist to ensure all aspects of the programme, qualification and the organisation are stated?

☐ Is time allocated during induction for information and discussion regarding equality and diversity, including policies, complaints and appeals?

☐ Can you include a workshop or session regarding equality and diversity, or include specialist speakers?

☐ Can you communicate with others who are involved with your students, for example teachers, workplace supervisors?

Designing learning

☐ Do your resources represent the diverse range of your students and local community?

☐ Do you need to adapt any resources to suit your students, for example the use of large print, coloured paper, etc.?

☐ Do you make reasonable adjustments to learning materials to ensure they are fully inclusive and do not draw attention to those requiring adjustments?

☐ Do you check all presentations, handouts, etc. to ensure they are legible and readable by all students, and don't contain too much jargon?

☐ Can you create extension activities to challenge higher level students or those who finish earlier?

☐ Can you make your teaching and learning materials accessible electronically?

☐ Do you need to obtain or arrange for any specialist equipment or support?

Facilitating learning

☐ Can you use a suitable inclusive icebreaker?

☐ Can you agree suitable ground rules with your students which include aspects of equality and diversity?

☐ Do you use a variety of stimulating teaching activities, methods and resources to cover all learning styles?

☐ Do you treat your students as individuals, using their names when possible?

☐ Can all students access the teaching environment, and use all relevant equipment and materials?

☐ Is your teaching environment conducive to learning, for example layout, accessibility?

☐ Is the language you use appropriate, non-discriminatory and at the right level?

☐ Do you manage discussions within the learning environment to ensure student language is appropriate and non-discriminatory?

☐ Do you make good use of occasions when naturally occurring opportunities occur regarding equality and diversity?

☐ Do you ensure individual student needs are met and differentiated for all abilities?

☐ Do you take into account all learning styles?

☐ Do you treat all students fairly?

☐ Do you ensure all students treat each other with respect and challenge negativity?

☐ Do you encourage teamwork?

☐ Do you present materials and topics in a way that are sensitive to equality and diversity?

☐ Can you build in sufficient time for group activities to advance equality and diversity, bearing in mind any cultural clashes that may occur?

☐ Is diversity included within your teaching and resources, for example referring to a variety of cultures, faiths, religions and traditions?

☐ Are people from diverse backgrounds, for example cultural, socioeconomic, people with disabilities, etc. visible in your resources?

☐ Can you confidently challenge prejudice, discrimination and stereotyping as it occurs?

☐ Can you put your own attitudes, values and beliefs behind if they conflict with your students or at the very least do not let them affect teaching and learning?

☐ Do you use appropriate body language and non-verbal communication?

☐ Can you refrain from touching students inappropriately, even to give support?

☐ Is equality and diversity an agenda item for meetings? Are meaningful topics discussed?

Assessing learning

☐ Is assessment planned with all students?

☐ Are appropriate assessment methods used for all students?

☐ Is assessment fair and not discriminative against any student?

☐ Can you use alternative forms of assessment, for example reading questions to a student who is visually impaired?

☐ Do you need to contact the awarding organisation to obtain extra time for assessments or exams due to language barriers or physical difficulties?

☐ Do you give feedback on an individual basis, giving developmental support where necessary, at a level to suit each student?

☐ Can you rephrase questions if they are not understood by the student?

☐ Do you differentiate for students' abilities and needs?

☐ Are your students aware of the appeals procedure?

☐ Are you keeping relevant records of progress?

Quality assurance and evaluation

☐ Do students have the opportunity to evaluate their programme in an anonymous way?

☐ Can all students understand the questions being asked, and complete the necessary forms? Can the forms be available electronically?

☐ Do you collect an adequate range of data including ethnicity, destinations, retention, achievement, progression, etc.?

☐ Do you analyse the data collected and do something positive with it?

☐ Can you follow up any feedback from students or others?

☐ Can you evaluate each session delivered and note any equality and diversity issues that naturally occurred?

☐ Can you foster links with the local community to improve your own knowledge?

☐ Can you take any further training to benefit yourself and your students?

INDEX